ASCLEPIADES
HIS LIFE AND WRITINGS

A TRANSLATION

of Cocchi's *Life of Asclepiades and*

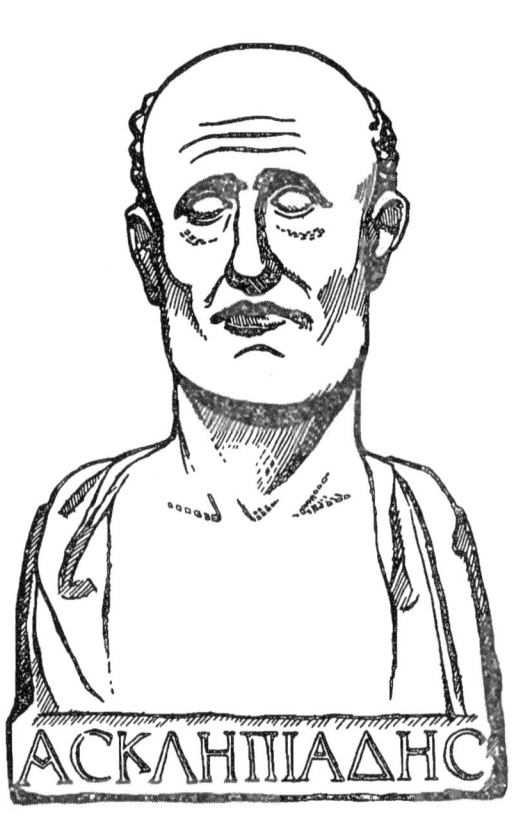

Elizabeth Licht, Publisher 195

360 Fountain Street, New Haven, Connecticu

Gumpert's *Fragments of Asclepiades*

ASCLEPIADES

HIS LIFE AND WRITINGS

by ROBERT MONTRAVILLE GREEN, M.D.

Emeritus Professor of Anatomy, Harvard Medical School,
Boston, Massachusetts

WAVERLY PRESS, INC.
BALTIMORE, MARYLAND

PRINTED IN THE UNITED STATES OF AMERICA

Dedicated To The Memory Of
Doctor Walter M. Solomon

Preface

In Ancient Greece many of the most competent physicians maintained some association with the national religion, either by affiliation with a temple to Asclepios or by assuming a name related to the mythical god of medicine. Thus scattered through Greek history ⁴ there have been forty men bearing the patronymic Asclepiades. The latest and most prominent of these was Asclepiades of Bithynia, born about three centuries after Hippocrates. He moved to Rome, where he practised medicine in the Golden Age of Cicero, Horace, and Virgil, two centuries before Galen.

Unhappily almost all his works have perished except for a few fragments. But from these, and from many contemporary references, Dr. Antonio Cocchi, who held the chair of Anatomy at the Royal Hospital of Santa Maria Nuova in Florence, wrote a "Life of Asclepiades" which appeared in 1762 in an English translation by an unknown hand, presumably from a previous Italian edition. This English version left much to be desired, and we asked the eminent linguist, Dr. Robert Montraville Green, to make a new translation from the Cocchi reprint published at Milan in 1824. In this volume, the eleventh of twelve discourses was the "Life of Asclepiades". Dr. Cocchi, who was born at Benevento on August 3, 1695, died at Florence on January 1, 1758.

Christian Gottlieb Gumpert while at the University of Weimar collected fragments of the writings of Asclepiades which he published in that city in 1794. At the time of this writing there is only one known extant copy of the Gumpert work in the Western Hemisphere, in the Surgeon-General's Library at Washington, from which this translation was made. Gumpert was quinquelingual, and since many of his references are from such authors as Aristotle, Democritus, Erasistratus, Herophilus, Celsus, Caelius Aurelianus, Dioscorides, Pliny, Ackerman, Bianchini, and Le Clerc, though his work is predominantly in Greek and Latin, there are some portions of the text in French, German, and Italian.

The "Fragments" presented here in English for the first time, along with a new translation of Cocchi's "Life", make Asclepiades available to many for the first time in more than a century. The historical importance of this fact is best appreciated when we recall that it was Asclepiades, who, as a founder of the Methodist Sect, summed up and transmitted the soundest traditions of his predecessors to the great Galen and thus preserved for us a priceless link in our heritage from Greek medical knowledge.

To Asclepiades many innovations have been attributed. He was the first to associate hydrophobia with the bite of rabid animals. He advocated walking on sand for paralysis, gave specific prescriptions of music for the mentally ill, used massage for muscle spasm as well as dry steaming and radiant heating. He considered man subject to physical laws and thus introduced philosophic theory into medical art. Not since 1841, when Ritter von Welz published at Würtzburg his "Des Asclepiades von Bithynien Gesundheitsvorschriften", has a book on this important physician been printed.

The bust of Asclepiades which is reproduced as the frontispiece now rests in the Capitoline Museum of Rome. It has never been fully established that this is the bust of "our Asclepiades", but most experts regard it as likely.

We note with great sorrow the death, on May 29, 1955, of the gentle scholar whose translation we are privileged to present in this volume.

SIDNEY LICHT, M.D.
New Haven, Connecticut

Table of Contents

Life of Asclepiades

Eleventh Discourse of Antonio Cocchi:
Concerning Asclepiades

"It would be all very well to despise these, if by seeking we could find none better and truer than they."

PLATO: Gorgias: LXXXII, 527.

"The inactive and ineffectual he seeks out for condemnation and removes it; but that which rouses and stimulates the understanding to something, he attracts; and those that tend to beauty of life itself, of these he makes the discussions that come to no use."

HIPPOCRATES.

Assuredly one of the most excellent and most fortunate men of antiquity, whose fame still endures in the world, was the physician Asclepiades, a Greek from the kingdom of Bithynia, who, about eighteen hundred years ago, cut a great figure at Rome in his art, of which he was, moreover, one of the most distinguished authorities.

Although at present all his works are lost, and there is no history of his life, it is our intention to investigate all the details available about his person and the practise of his profession.

The name Asclepiades, which in its origin means son or descendant of Asclepios, was borne anciently by many, either singly and personally, or combined as a cognomen and given for special praise to physicians, or assumed by some from a certain vanity of respectable, though false, genealogy, as if they were descended from that imaginary personage called Asclepios, anciently considered by the poets as representing that part of the uncomprehended power of nature which sometimes causes spontaneous disappearance of diseases and was therefore recognized as a god and thence commonly worshipped by the most cultivated nations as long as the false polytheistic theology prevailed among them.

Our Asclepiades had such a name in its first and simplest significance of indicating solely his own personality. And because there are encountered in books more than forty other Asclepiades, great and small, it is a proper precaution not to confound one or another of them with ours, as has befallen some scholars. He should be distinguished either by having the bare name, as if he were the most celebrated of all, or by the addition of Bithynian, or of physician, or of circumstances relative to him alone.

Of the twenty-seven ancient writers in whom any mention of him is found, so far as comes to our knowledge, eleven are Greek and sixteen Latin. The Greeks are five physicians,—Cassius,[1] Erotianus,[2] Galen,[3] Oribasius,[4] and Aetius;[5] three philosophers,—Plutarch,[6]

[1] Cassius, Felix: B.C. 63 to A.D. 37 Author of Ἰατρικαὶ Ἀπορίαι καὶ Προβλήματαν φυσικά
[2] Erotianus: A.D. 37–68. Author of Τῶν παρ' Ἱπποκράτει Λέξεων Συναγωγή
[3] Galen: A.D. 130–200. Author of 83 extant genuine, 19 doubtful, and 45 spurious works
[4] Oribasius· A.D. 325–395. Author of Συναγωγαὶ Ἰατρικαὶ Σύνοψις in 9 books, and Εὐπόριστα in 4 books.
[5] Aetius A.D. 475–525. Author of Βιβλία Ἰατρικὰ Ἑκκαίδεκα
[6] Plutarch: A.D. 50 to 125. Author of 46 Lives and of 60 other works (Moralia and Apophthegms).

Sextus,[7] and Stobaeus;[8] two geographers,—Strabo[9] and Stephanus;[10] and one theologian, Eusebius.[11]

The Latins are five physicians,—Celsus,[12] Scribonius,[13] Aurelianus,[14] Marcellus,[15] and Theodorus;[16] three philosophers,—Cicero,[17] Seneca,[18] and Chalcidius;[19] six miscellaneous,—Pliny,[20] Apuleius,[21] Censorinus,[22] Macrobius,[23] Marcianus,[24] and Cassiodorus;[25] and two theologians,—the supposed Clement,[26] translated by Rufinus, and Tertullian.[27]

[7] Sextus Empiricus: A.D. 200–250. Author of Πυῤῥώνιαι Ὑποτυπώσεις ἤ Σκεπτικὰ Ὑπομνήματα in 3 books; and Πρὸς τοὺς Μαθηματικούς in 11 books.

[8] Stobaeus: A.D. 425–475. Author of 'Εκλογαὶ φυσικαὶ διαλεκτικαὶ καὶ 'Ηθικαί and of 'Ανθολόγιον.

[9] Strabo: B.C. 54–A.D. 24: Author of 'Ιστορικὰ Ὑπομνήματα in 43 books and of Τεωγράφικα in 17 books.

[10] Stephanus: A.D. 410–500. Author of 'Εθνικά, a geographical lexicon.

[11] Eusebius Pamphili: A.D. 264–340. Author of Χρονικὰ Παντοδαπῆς 'Ιστορίας. He was Bishop of Caesarea from 315 A.D.

[12] A. Cornelius Celsus: B.C. 63 to A.D. 37. Author of De Medicina in 8 books.

[13] Scribonius Largus: B C. 42 to A.D. 54. Roman physician and author.

[14] Caelius Aurelianus: A D. 300–400. Author of De Morbis Acutis, in 3 books and De Morbis Chronicis in 5 books.

[15] Nonius Marcellus: A.D. 350–450. Author of De Compendiosa Doctrina per Litteras ad Filium.

[16] Theodorus of Rhodes: B.C. 63 to A.D. 37. Eminent as a rhetorician. A native of Gadara, east of Jordan.

[17] Marcus Tullius Cicero: B.C. 106 to 43. Greatest of all Roman orators and prose authors.

[18] Lucius Annaeus Seneca: A.D. 1–65. Greatest of all Roman philosophers.

[19] Chalcidius: A D. 500–600. Author of a Latin translation and commentary of Plato.

[20] C. Plinius Secundus, the elder, born in A.D. 23, died in the eruption of Vesuvius in A.D. 79. He was author of the Historia Naturalis in 37 books.

[21] Apuleius of Madura: born in A D. 130. Author of I. Metamorphoseon seu de Asino Aureo. II. Floridorum Libri. III. De Deo Socratis. IV. De Dogmate Platonis. V. De Mundo. VI. Apologia sive de Magia Liber.

[22] Caius Censorinus: an eminent orator, and leader of the Marian party in the first century B.C.

[23] Ambrosius Aurelius Theodosius Macrobius: a grammarian of the fourth century A.D. Author of I. Saturnalia Conviviorum. II. Commentary on Cicero's Dream of Scipio, to which we owe the source of Chaucer's Parlement of Fowles III. De Differentiis et Societatibus Graeci Latinique Verbi.

[24] Marcianus Mineus Felix Capella: a native of Carthage in the fifth century A.D. Author of an encyclopaedia in 9 books, much esteemed in the Middle Ages.

[25] Magnus Aurelius Cassiodorus: A.D. 468–568. Governed the Ostrogothic Kingdom under Theodoric the Great. Author of I. Variorum Epistolarum Libri XII. II. Chronicon. III. De Orthographia. IV. De Arte Grammatica. V. De Artibus ac Disciplinis Liberalium Litterarum. VI. De Anima. VII. De Rebus Gestis Gothorum.

[26] Clemens Alexandrinus: A.D. 193–221. Author of I. Hortatory Address to the Greeks. II. Pedagogy. III. Stromata.

[27] Quintus Septimius Florens Tertullianus: A.D. 160–240. Author of an Apologia or Defence of Christianity.

In some of the references of these, there are also found citations from ten other authors, nine Greek and one Latin, whose works are now lost, so far as they spoke of him. Five of these were physicians,—Athenaeus Attalensis,[28] (founder of the sect of the Pneumatists), Menodotus Empiricus,[29] Metrodorus,[30] Moschion,[31] and Soranus;[32] two were philosophers,—Antiochus[33] and Athenodorus,[34] preceptors, the former of Cicero, the latter of Augustus; two historians,—Varro[35] and Herennius Philo;[36] and one a theologian,—Dionysius,[37] Bishop of Alexandria.

Of the aforesaid twenty-seven extant ancient writers, only four have spoken about him at any great length. The first and oldest of these is the Roman, Cornelius Celsus. Though not a physician himself by profession, Celsus, assisted by Greek books and perhaps by some competent physician as his friend, composed a complete treatise on medicine in his own language, very simple in style but beautiful in its purity, with accuracy and judgment; so that, having been preserved until our times, it is considered now as the first and the best book among all the ancient Latins pertaining to medicine. And because its merit depends principally on the opinions which it reports of the lost authors, which at his time were complete and commonly read, perhaps for that reason his contemporary Roman writers, like Columella[38] and Quintilian,[39] have praised him spar-

[28] Athenaeus, a famous physician, born at Attalia in Cilicia, practised at Rome in the first century A.D.

[29] Menodotus: a physician of Nicomedia in Bithynia, pupil of Antiochus of Laodicea, tutor to Herodotus of Tarsus; an empiric of the second century A.D.

[30] Metrodorus of Stratonice in Caria, was at first a disciple of Epicurus, but later attached himself to the school of Carneades. Flourished about 10 B.C.

[31] Moschion, author of a Greek treatise on Gynaecology. Lived at Rome in the second century A D.

[32] Soranus of Ephesus, practised medicine at Alexandria and Rome, A.D. 98–138.

[33] Antiochus of Ascalon, friend of Lucullus, taught Cicero at Athens B.C. 79.

[34] Athenodorus of Tarsus: taught the young Octavius at Apollonia in Epirus.

[35] Caius Terentius Varro, most learned of the Romans, born in B.C. 116, died B.C. 28. Author of 490 books, of which only two are extant, De Rustica and De Lingua Latina.

[36] Herennius Philo of Tarsus in Cilicia, a celebrated physician frequently quoted by Galen.

[37] Dionysius the Areopagite, one of the early fathers of the Church, converted by St. Paul's preaching at Athens.

[38] Lucius Junius Moderatus Columella: born in Spain, resided at Rome in the first century A.D. Author of De Rustica, a work on agriculture in 12 books, still extant. Also De Arboribus, in one book.

[39] Marcus Fabius Quintilianus: A.D. 40–118, most celebrated of Roman rhetoricians. His great work is his De Institutione Oratoria in 12 books. He is also author of 164 declamationes, originally 388 in number.

ingly, and Pliny has not made any account of his medical work, where, not recalling him, he says that very few Romans had touched such a subject, and that these had written in Greek.* Celsus, then, confesses in general to have followed Asclepiades in many things; and if, sometimes, he is not of the same opinion, he states the reason therefor with decent respect.

The second author who speaks much of Asclepiades is Pliny, a courtier, soldier, and administrator, who, for his own diversion wrote a large book of Natural History, which contains a prodigious medley of information, both physical, moral, and historical, extracted, as he himself attests, from about two thousand books, which now are almost all lost, which is the reason why his has become more important for us.

It is true that, when these statements of Pliny have been examined in many ways by experts, it has been found that many do not turn out exactly accurate, and that it is expedient to use them with great caution. Particularly it is to be observed that he wished to meddle much with medicine, which he had never practised nor fundamentally understood, since it was clearly declared by him† the only one of the Greek arts not yet exercised with the Roman seriousness. He pretends to reveal its mysteries by transferring some recipes from the Greek books, and thinks thus to make useless the professors of that nation, against whom, it is not known why, he had always shown a certain ignoble envy and a desire to debase their authority as much as he can. This he has done particularly against Asclepiades, although the latter had died a long time before; unless it may be believed that, since his statements are rarely original, he had copied some writer contemporary with that great man and, as is wont to happen, envious and spiteful towards him. But nevertheless we ought to be grateful to Pliny for some particulars which, without him, would have remained unknown like the rest: it is up to us to draw from them the correct conclusions.

The third author who reports many data about Asclepiades, for the most part disapprovingly, is Caelius Aurelianus, from the city of Sicca in Africa, by whom we have a Treatise of Medicine in crude and barbarous Latin, in which he professes himself as a translator of Soranus, who flourished at the beginning of the second

* H.N. XXIX, cap. I., P. 5, 8 p. 669.
† H.N. LVI.

century after Christ. He is valuable for the quotations which he makes from lost authors, but for his own sake not of much worth. To judge by his style, he appears of the fifth century; but from his sentences and quotations he could be believed somewhat older.

The fourth is Galen at the end of the second century, who is known for his fluency and for his misfortune of having often wrongly criticized the most illustrious physicians since Hippocrates; so that the chief merit of his books consists similarly in the fragments of the ancients whom he quotes, for the most part to confute them. Often enough he does this honor to Asclepiades, whom he considers in other respects as ingenious, learned and highly eloquent, though opposed to his own peripatetic theories. Anyone may perceive the disadvantage of having to take information from unfavorable testimony; but since these things cannot be otherwise, it behoves us to make use of all the factual information which comes furnished to us by the tradition of the ancients, whatever was their intention, provided the inalienable right is not lost of judging matters of reason according to the dictates of our own conscience.

Besides his fame and the testimony of these authors, there remains also of Asclepiades a beautiful antique bust, intact and on display to public view in the magnificent collection of the Campidoglio of Rome, bare-headed, with his hair short, and without a beard, with a cloak in likeness of a Greek sage, and with Greek letters on the square antique base, portraying his name. This bust about forty years ago was buried within the walls of Rome, near the Porta Capena, where perhaps anciently it served as a scholarly ornament for some portico or library or school or other edifice of that principal region of the city, which occupied that site. And having been diligently observed in all its material circumstances and by all the rules of antiquarian criticism, it was justly attributed, by the experts who have described it,* to our Asclepiades, rather than to any other of the same name, but not of so great fame and merit.

From this bust, and from seeing in Pliny[40] that Varro spoke of Asclepiades, without stating in which of his many books, it might perhaps be conjectured that that Father of Roman Learning had

---

* Blas Caryophil. diss. miscell. Rom. 1718, p. 331; and Io. Bottari Mus Capitolin. tom I. tav. 3. Rom 1741 and 1750.

[40] H.N. XXVI, Cap 3, P. 8, where Arduenus conjectures that the surname of Asclepiades was Dosipsychron; rather that it ought to be called Psychrodotes.

given him a place in his curious work, which is lost, of the "Images" or of the "Hundred Weeks", in which he collected the portraits of seven hundred illustrious men whose busts were wont to be placed in libraries, adding for each an epigram of his own, as is inferred from Pliny[41] himself and from the Letters of Symmachus,[42] in whose time,—that is, at the end of the fourth century,—these eulogies were still extant.

With the authority of these documents alone there must be re-traced the deeds and opinions of this worthy physician, combining the scattered evidences and deducing from them the most probable conjectures. First, we need to fix, with the greatest possible accuracy, the time in which he lived among men.

The ancient authors, who in general were much less accurate in chronology than we, furnish us only some such sign whence springs doubt rather than certainty. Pliny says that he lived in the time of Pompey;[43] which is found repeated by almost all the moderns who have cared to speak of him, which expression, although too vague, it seems ought to be understood of the adult age of Pompey, when he was the principal person of the Roman name; and this epoch could not even begin much before his twenty-eighth year, just after the death of Sulla, which was in the year of Rome 676 A.U.C.

But the authority of Cicero[44] leads us to believe that Asclepiades was somewhat older, and that he belonged rather to the age pre-ceding Pompey; since in the dialogue of the Orator he makes Lucius Crassus speak of him as already deceased. Now this dialogue, although it was written by Cicero when he was fifty-two years old, that is in the year of Rome 628 A.U.C., was nevertheless assumed as if having occurred in the consulship of Philippus, that is in 633 A.U.C., when he was still a youngster of fifteen years; so that, not having been present at it himself, it was related to him afterwards by Cotta, who was one of the interlocutors and who died in 680 A.U.C. (73 B.C.).

In this dialogue, then, Cicero does not speak in his own person, but in that of Lucius Licinius Crassus, in whose villa it is supposed that this discourse occurred. To this Crassus, a senator distinguished

---

[41] H.N. XXXV, Cap. 2, P. 2, p. 175.

[42] Symmachi Epist. I, 4.

[43] H N. XXVI, cap 3, P. 7, p. 444.

[44] De Oratore I, 62.

for his eloquence and for his political knowledge, who was then forty-nine years old and who died a few months later, he ascribes many things alluding to the circumstances of those times; and among other men of merit he makes him mention Asclepiades as having been already his physician and friend and that of many noble and virtuous characters, among whom were Lucius Mucius Scaevola, the augur, already fairly aged and a highly esteemed attorney, and Marcus Antonius, an eloquent orator, who died four years later, and who was grandfather of the famous Marcus. So it is not credible that, if Asclepiades had been then alive or had survived thereafter, Cicero would have wished to commit a superfluous anachronism, not being accustomed to take such licenses as Plato has often taken in his Dialogues, which he purposely wished to make much more like drama. Whereas Cicero, on many occasions, declares himself to be a scrupulous observer of propriety and probability, which he has well maintained in the other parts of this same dialogue.

Therefore the knowledge of Asclepiades should be attributed to the personages introduced, and not to Cicero himself, who was then much too young, although it has been attributed to him by almost all the moderns who have mentioned Asclepiades. And because Pompey was still some months younger than Cicero, it does not seem that the expression of Cicero, which places Asclepiades in the age of Pompey, can be preserved otherwise than by understanding it of the first fifteen years of his life. But since this does not seem to be the natural sense of that phrase, it may be suspected rather that this is one of the customary chronological inaccuracies of Pliny, and that perhaps he supposed Asclepiades to be of the time of Pompey because he had seen some of the consultations or of the medical books consigned by him to King Mithridates, whose defeat and total extinction had been the most glorious exploit of that magnanimous Roman, Pompey.

Moreover, these very books from Asclepiades to Mithridates, and the invitations of that king, sent to him by means of his ambassadors at Rome, which Asclepiades did not wish to accept, as Pliny[45] himself indicates, furnish another evidence that this physician was sufficiently advanced and well established at Rome and already famous throughout the world many years before Pompey;

[45] H.N. VII, cap. 37.

since it is not credible that there would have been this negotiation of ambassadors unless before Mithridates alienated himself from the friendship of the Romans and finally declared himself their open and implacable enemy, which, according to history, he seems to have done about the year of Rome 660 A.U.C. And it is credible that the ambassadors of this superlatively powerful prince, who Pliny says were scorned by that physician, were not sent purposely on so frivolous a commission; but that this private affair was transacted by someone of those who had been dispatched by him to Rome on various occasions, chiefly in the preceding ten years: and perhaps they were the same ones who, in the year 652, came there with much money, and were suspected, as Diodorus Siculus[46] relates, of being commissioned to solicit with it also certain noble senators.

Another indication of the age of Asclepiades is supplied by Sextus Empiricus,* who quotes a passage from Antiochus† Academicus, who was a celebrated professor of philosophy at Athens, and in part contemporary with the same Asclepiades, taken from the second of the books by him entitled the Canonicals, which must have treated of the canons or rules of the art of reasoning, and of the nature and operations of the human mind, or, as should now be said, of metaphysics.

In this passage Antiochus cites the opinion of Asclepiades, as of a man of the greatest reputation, but already dead. Now this book being, as appears and as Sextus also supposes, in the Sect of the Academici, shows it to have been composed before that philosopher went over to Stoicism and disputed against the Academici themselves.

But already he was disputing against them, when he found himself at Alexandria in the company of Lucius Lucullus, who had been despatched there from Attica, as ambassador to the King Ptolomey VIII, by Sulla, supreme commander of the Mithridatic War. These Alexandrine philosophic disputes, then, of which the Roman ambassador made his amusement in the intervals of his actual labors, will follow the year of Rome 667 A.U.C., as Cicero makes Lucullus himself relate, in the Dialogue bearing his name, which is the fourth

---

[46] Excerptae Legationes, tom. II, P. 34, p. 631.

* Adversus Logicos, VII, P. 201, p. 412.

† Of Ascalon, founder of the Fifth Academy.

book of the Academic Questions; whence it can be argued that Asclepiades was already dead some months before; and therefore it will seem a fairly moderate and reasonable supposition to fix the death of Asclepiades at the latest possible date compatible with the evidence of Crassus taken from Cicero.

And because this dialogue of the Orator is supposed to have oc-curred in the days of the Roman games, that is in September, it can be affirmed without danger of very great error, that Asclepiades died in that same year, 663 A.U.C.; since it is known, moreover, from Pliny that he had raught extreme old age, and that his death was expedited by a casual fall, we will say that he might then be a little more than eighty years old: so that, counting so much back-wards, his birth could be placed at about the year of Rome 580 A.U.C., which is the second year of the one hundred and fifty-first Olympiad and 174 years before the Christian dispensation now as commonly adopted and employed.

Some modern men of letters declare with the most learned Fabricius* that Asclepiades lived a hundred and fifty years; but that does not seem credible, both on account of the intrinsic im-probability of such a completely unusual natural event, as also the deep silence about it which is encountered among the ancients.

Of the places in which Asclepiades passed some part of his long life, there are found named only four cities and one province. First, it appears that he was born at Cios in the kingdom of Bithynia, which occupied the northern part of Asia Minor opposite the ex-tremity of Europe, and the site where now is Constantinople. This is gathered from the only sign given of it by the author of the Intro-duction to Medicine among the works of Galen,[47] where Asclepiades is called Bithynian and Cian and also Prusan. From the ancient geographers it is known that Cios, having been restored by King Prusias, was called Prusa, and that, being situated in the western shore on the Propontis, it was distinct from another Prusa of the same kingdom of Bithynia, on the river Hippius, near the northern shore on the Pontus, and was distinct also from Prusa near Mount Olympus. The Prusa from which Asclepiades was called Prusan

---

* Bibl. Gr. Vi, cap. 9, p. 87 *Elench. med. vet* on the authority of *Longaville. Harcuet* in the History of the Long-Lived *Mém. de Trevoux,* 1718, *October,* p. 639 *Corsini Syllab. phil.* p. XXVI, preface to Plutarch *de plac. Phil.* on the authority of Fabricius

[47] Tom. IV, p. 372, where, instead of Cian, is read Cianian, as in the other editions.

never wholly lost its old name of Cios, perhaps because, being a Greek city, maritime, mercantile, and populous, it retained in its government some semblance of a republic.

Polybius[48]* and his successor Livy[49]† inform us that it was protected by the Roman senate and liberated from the jurisdiction of King Prusias in the famous treaty of peace of the Romans with King Philip of Macedon in the year of Rome 558 A.U.C., twenty-two years before the supposed birth of Asclepiades; and it is seen that the Cians, in the various vicissitudes of all Bithynia, preserved, until the end of the third Christian century, some shadow of their liberty; there being found at any rate some coins of theirs, struck with the heads of the Emperors, and, among the last, of Decius and of Gallus.

Having been born a citizen of this republic, it is found that he also lived some time at Parium, also a Greek maritime city of the Propontis and free, although under the protection of the King of Pergamos, sovereign of the surrounding country. The abode of Asclepiades in this city, as also in other neighboring ones of the Hellespont, is inferred from some medical observations made there by him and related by Aurelianus and Oribasius.[50] In the same way it is known that he also lived for some time at Athens.

And finally it is known, from the relation of almost all the authors who speak of him, that he passed the greater part of his time in Rome, and that there he ended his days. And because from the testimony of Pliny[51] it appears that in Rome he was chiefly known, more for his learning and eloquence than for his medicine, it may be conjectured that he went there in his youth, and thus it may be supposed that he remained in his own country until about the age

[48] Legazione IX, p. 1106.

[49] XXXIII, cap. 30.

* Polybius was born B C. 204 at Megalopolis in Arcadia. He wrote a history of the world in forty books, beginning at B.C. 220, where his predecessor, Aratus, had left off, and ending at 146 B.C. with the destruction of Corinth. The first seventeen books are extant and nearly intact, the remainder have perished except for fragments. He also wrote "The Life of Philopoimen," "A Treatise on Tactics," and "A History of the Murantine War." He died B.C. 122 by a fall from his horse.

† Titus Livius was born at Patavium in B.C. 59, and died there in A.D. 17. He wrote a history of Rome from its foundation until B.C. 9. in 142 books, of which 35 are extant and complete, the remainder survive only in epitomes.

[50] In Niceta's Collection, p. 155, P. XII.

[51] H.N. XXVI, cap. 3.

of twenty years, that he studied and travelled in various places until thirty, and that a little later he established himself at Rome, where he continued to enjoy his fame for perhaps more than fifty years, coming thus to complete that octogenarian span which, on the authority of the ancients, we have attributed to him.

Of his parentage, or of his ancestors, or of his descendants we have no information, although Reinesius,[52] most learned physician and antiquarian of the past century, by spontaneous conjecture alone induced himself to believe that a certain Caius Calpurnius Asclepiades, a physician of whom there is found a most honorable ancient inscription of the times of the Emperor Hadrian, might have been a countryman and perhaps a grandson of our Asclepiades.

Although the twenty-seven ancient writers who speak of him have kept silent about his condition, it appears that it may be conjectured that in his country he was of the middle or citizen class, every people being naturally distinguished into three classes, whatever may be the disposition of its laws. By the concordant testimony of all the aforesaid writers it is known that Asclepiades was very learned in the knowledge of words and of things and that he was the foremost physician of his century in the leading city of the world, retaining there, as it appears, his single name, in the Greek manner, without needing or caring to assume, through clientage or through other dependency, that of some Roman family, as many other Greeks have done. He was content to be the humble friend of those powerful senators, who were like so many kings in their magnanimity.

From all these circumstances it can be inferred with assurance that in his earliest age he must have had a very liberal education, and that therefore he was not of a very humble family, as Leonardo di Capua[53] asserts, misunderstanding the passage of Pliny,[54] where he marvels "that a single man," (these are his own words), "from a most trivial nation, setting himself to the undertaking without management and without power, had been able to give the laws of health to the self-styled human race"

But it is clearly seen that Pliny means here to allude to the nation of the Greeks, whom the proud Romans called a vain and frivolous

[52] *Inscript. antiq.* classis XI, 4, p. 608.
[53] Ragionam, V. p. 366.
[54] H.N. XXVI, cap. 3, P. VIII, p. 445.

people, considering them occupied solely in the fine arts, in the sciences, in poetry, in oratory, in luxury and in lust, and seeing lost among them the power and the will to fight and to conquer. And truly there did not endure long among the Greeks that for which, according to Thucydides,* Pericles praised the Athenians, that is for being magnificent, pleasure-loving, of good taste in all the arts, sound reasoners and philosophers, and at the same time sturdy, tireless, discreet and courageous warriors.

However, it does not appear that the mediocrity of the circum-stances of Asclepiades removed his possibility of being well off in paternal goods, since he was able in youth to apply himself to his studies, to travel through Greece, to enjoy life at Athens and to acquire polish there, adding to his abilities the knowledge of the various systems of philosophy, and finally having been able to make his way to Rome and establish himself, things which can not be done without money.

After having been recognized as the best physician at Rome, as all agree that he was, that he should be able to make a great fortune is very likely; since experience demonstrates that nothing is easier than to acquire immense wealth by being an able and esteemed physician in a city where studied luxury is cultivated and parsimony is abhorred, provided this city is densely populous and opulent, as Rome was in those times, perhaps to excess; especially since the riches of human commerce were then incomparably greater and commoner than in the centuries nearer us, and since there was anciently an exorbitant magnificance in the fees of physicians, as may be inferred from the complaints of Pliny and the testimony of other ancients. And it is not impossible that Asclepiades, being beloved and esteemed by the most considerable personages in Rome, in order to free himself from the inconveniences of being a foreigner, had obtained Roman citizenship or, as they said, the right of the Quirites, as, about a hundred years before, had been granted to Archagathus, who was the first Greek physician that had arrived at Rome. On this supposition, we must believe that the gentile name and first name which he assumed have gone into oblivion. But nevertheless there is no objection to supposing that, since no trace is found of a Roman name adopted by him, and since the toga is

* Hist. II, P. 38 et sq. Thucydides was born at Athens in 471 B.C. and died in 401 B.C. He wrote an 8-volume history of Greece, primarily of the Peloponnesian War.

not seen on his statue, he did not dread the dangers of alienship, feeling himself to be of an innocent nature and without ambition.

Regarding his personal qualities, in the first place his continuous and excellent good health up to extreme old age is amply attested by Pliny, never having had any illness, and having finally died from the external occasion of a blow in a fall; whence it may be inferred that the primary warps of his body were naturally robust, and his organs well composed and his humors of optimum mixture. Being aware of this himself, and hoping to be able to preserve his health by his temperance and by his skill in the art which he possessed, it may be that he sometimes jokingly, never in earnest, said or wrote what Pliny* reports seriously, that he hazarded with fortune all his fame, if he should ever get sick in any way. And it appears that it is only a reflection of Pliny's, which he adds, that Asclepiades having won this wager by dying not of sickness but of a fall, this contributed to the high esteem of him which remained also after his death.

It appears that his form was decorous and majestic, as can be conjectured from his aforesaid statue, in semblance of a sexagenarian man, of slender stature and with a countenance both pensive and tranquil.

Just as the true sensations, on which are founded the functions and operations of the mind, depend much on the health and on the vigor and regulated motion of the organs, it is no wonder if also the genius, which is no other than the inner faculty of thinking, was great in Asclepiades, as is argued by the ability which he acquired in the natural sciences and in various branches of learning, and as is much more securely deduced from the truth which is finally found in the greater part of his propositions, as they appear in the scanty and scattered fragments of his works, although they were in his time, and have been for many centuries afterwards, contrary to the opinions commonly current.

It appears that he had by nature a fairly prompt faculty of apprehending or clearly conceiving ideas, and of retaining them completely, and of distinguishing them exactly, that is of seeing also the slightest differences in them; in which operations the in-

* H.N. VII, cap. 37, P 37, p 59 It appears that this passage, misunderstood, induced Boerhaave to say that Asclepiades, utilizing his robustness to increase his reputation as a fine physician, boasted of having the secrets of postponing disease and prolonging life. *Praelect. Acad.* P. XIV, *prolegom.* p. 22.

tellect is rather passive. But at the same time it appears that he was very active and strong and acute in combining or uniting his concepts, and in reawakening or recalling to his memory the most opportune imaginations, and in seeking out the most remote and recondite but connected conclusions. The mind being active in these combinations, its excellence is more wont to be distinguished, not only because one man is more active, penetrating, and perspicacious than another, but, which is more important, by a certain sense of truth which some have remarkably fine and delicate by nature, and by a certain pure natural desire to discover it where it is most concealed, and by that magnanimous universal benevolence which some few more lofty spirits display in disclosing their scientific observations also to the public, who are for the most part ungrateful and malicious listeners.

That such was the genius of Asclepiades, lively in its imaginations of likenesses and of examples which render its eloquence clear and pleasing, and that at the same time he was judicious and profound and veracious in his reasoning, so far as comported with the discoveries of his century, cannot be doubted by anyone willing to examine candidly the remains of his works, free from the reflections of those who report them.

That he began his studies from earliest youth in his own country, before passing from Asia to Europe, is very credible, because he always possessed certain faculties which are not observed in those who set themselves late to learning. Such are principally the style correct, clear, and elegant; the reasoning sagacious, inventive, and exact; and a passionate sense for natural truths, for the acquisition of which abilities Bithynia, with its neighboring countries, was at that time particularly opportune, on account of its many Greek cities of Attic origin, in which, since the best language was spoken, was established and extended a taste for oratory, not forensic and seditious, but philosophic and tranquil, for dissertations of varied argument, of which many Bithynian writers are found mentioned, and some have still remained who show the succession of Asiatic eloquence more luxuriant and lively until the second century after Christ, like Dion the Prusan[55] and Aelius Aristides,[56] when the powerful rhetoric of Athens was already extinct.

[55] A.D. 155 to 230.
[56] A.D. 117 to 180.

It may be believed that in the age of Asclepiades there remained in the schools of Bithynia, of the Hellespont, of Mysia, and of Phrygia, the successors of the famous men mentioned by Strabo and natives of these parts, grammarians, dialecticians, orators, historians; and, what was more important, he might know and hear the two illustrious Bithynian mathematicians, Hipparchus[57] and Theodosius.[58] Certain it is that it appears from his fragments that he employed the Attic dialect and that the proper characteristic of his style was clarity; and from his exact manner of deducing the necessary conclusions from his premises, in which Galen himself says[59] that he was excellent, it may be surmised that he had practised sufficiently in a course of geometry, from the study of which is learned, better than in any other way, the art of demonstration, as Galileo has indicated.

In philosophy Bithynia was supplied by the schools of Epicurus who, even if he did not really liberate Greece from stupidity, as the poet Menander[60] sings of him, at least revived the taste for natural science, restoring to light some of the opinions of the old physicists, especially of Anaxagoras[61] and of Democritus,[62] and bringing men back to the search for the mechanical causes of the perceptible appearances of things, from the consideration of which they had been somewhat removed by the three other most celebrated schools, Platonic, Peripatetic, and Stoic.

Asclepiades, who had chosen medicine for his profession, perceived well that, just as the dramatic inventions of Plato could have their use in certain occurrences, and the logical subtleties of Aristotle could entertain scholastic wits and geniuses, and the rigid severity of Zeno well suited the most important business of the legislature, so, for a purely experimental art, that philosophy was supremely opportune which universally preferred sense to imagination.

In the schools of Bithynia there should have remained still more

[57] B C. 160 to 100.

[58] Mentioned by Strabo and Vitruvius.

[59] Concerning the Natural Faculties, lib I, tom. I, p. 94.

[60] Menander, B C. 342 to 291, leader of the New Comedy at Athens. He wrote 100 plays, of which only fragments are extant, though Terence translated and imitated them. "Epicurus rescued Greece from unreason."

[61] Anaxagoras: B.C. 500 to 428, a philosopher of the Ionian School. He considered mind (nous) the cause of all things.

[62] Democritus: B.C. 460 to 361. Father of the Atomic Theory.

in credit at the time of Asclepiades the opinions of Epicurus[63] who, a little more than a hundred years before, in the city of Lampsacus,[64] in the flower of his youth, had made the second demonstration of his doctrines; and in the stay of four years, which he then made there, he acquired the esteem and affection of that people; so that, as Strabo* observes, he always considered that city thereafter as another fatherland of his, and among those citizens found his best friends and most illustrious disciples: whence he often made return there for his diversion and comfort.

Bithynia provided Asclepiades another favorable occasion for the best choice of the Sect of medicine to which he chiefly devoted himself. This was that of the Herophileans, from the famous Herophilus, a citizen of Chalcedon in that same province, who lived about four generations before him, and was a great and perhaps the first human anatomist, a favorite of the magnificent Ptolemy, founder of the Greek monarchy of Egypt. Of the followers of this Herophilus there was a distinguished and great school in the vicinity of Laodicea in Phrygia, as Strabo informs us, with which province the city of Cios, which was not far distant, had an established and most advantageous commerce, as Mela† asserts.

And it is credible that Asclepiades had some relations with this school, since Alexander Philalethes, an illustrious physician, who, Strabo says, was president of it at his time, is known, by the authority of two medical writers, Aurelian and Theodorus, to have had Asclepiades for his master. Experience also demonstrates that the mere residence of able men in a country scatters there the seeds of many doctrines, which for some generations maintain themselves there as common and familiar ideas, as if by tradition: as it is seen that among ourselves the teachings and sayings have not yet vanished of Galileo, Borelli, Steno, Malpighi, Redi, and Bellini, with whom our ancestors lived familiarly.

Bithynia was besides most opportune for the youthful medical studies of Asclepiades on account of the marvellous and fortunate

[63] Born 342 B C. in Samos, resided later at Athens, Colophon, and Mytilene He wrote 300 volumes, which have all perished except a few fragments found at Herculaneum; but Lucretius' "de Rerum Natura" is based on them He died in his garden at Athens in 270 B C.

[64] Lampsacus was a city of Mysia on the shore of the Hellespont, famous for wine.

* Strabo· B C 54 to A D. 24 He wrote a Geography in 17 books, and refers to Epicurus in XIII, p. 590

† Pomponius Mela, a Roman geographer of the first century A D.

situation of those countries of Asia, with so great a variety of seas and lands and of numerous cities of differing government, both Greek and barbarian, all populous, rich, sumptuous, erudite, with commerce to west and north by sea, with all the coasts of the Mediterranean and of the Pontus, and to the east by land through the heart of Phrygia with all the other more remote realms of blissful Asia; so that it is no wonder that Caesar and Augustus should sometimes think of placing there the centre of the Roman Empire.

Thus Asclepiades, from his early youth, might easily acquire experience of the great variety of temperaments and customs of people, and that skill of natural history which are seen to shine through in the fragments of his works among the very drugs which he rejects, and enter into the true spirit of botany, as Dioscorides[65] indicates while admonishing his followers to take more pains with the descriptions of the herbs, which are taken from the truth, than with their virtues, which are for the most part false and imaginary; and precisely thus it is wont to be done in our century, in which this study has been exalted to a high degree.

In anatomy, as is seen in his aforesaid fragments, it appears that he made dissections of animals, not being able, perhaps, to make them in human cadavera, which in all ancient governments were sacred and inviolable. It has been found that only Herophilus and Erasistratus among their contemporaries enjoyed the advantage of being able to dissect a good number of cadavera of condemned criminals, by concession of two scholarly and valorous kings of the school of Alexander the Great, and after his death founders of two most beautiful realms, Ptolemy of Egypt, who had with him Herophilus, and Seleucus of Syria, who retained Erasistratus at his court with a most ample salary, as Appian[66] states.

Asclepiades made use of the human anatomies of these two distinguished physicians, assuming them true and exact, especially of Herophilus, his countryman and authority. As for medicine, it is manifest that Asclepiades studied it from youth and in Asia; because in his very fragments are found practical observations, rare and important, made by himself in Parium and in the Hellespont, of

---

[65] Dioscorides Pedanias: 100–200 A D. Materia medica, in 5 books. I pref. p. 1. He was born at Anazarba in Cilicia.

[66] Appianus born at Alexandria and lived at Rome in the second century A D. He wrote a history of Rome in 24 books, of which eleven are still extant

certain particulars which are not obvious to any but the most skillful, and for which the philosopher Antiochus, who knew him at Athens, calls him a physician second to none other.

So that Pliny's statement has the appearance of invidious detraction, that Asclepiades suddenly planted himself at Rome to practise medicine, without having first learned it, having only a sagacious genius and eloquence, of which he had been a teacher there.

It can well be that at the beginning of his residence in that city, eager to learn and then just beginning to understand the arts of thinking and speaking, to introduce himself he taught to the young nobility some branch of the Greek learning in which he was proficient; but it is too gross an inference to deduce from his ability that he lacked the other, which had been the principal object of his studies and travels. It had already been sagely observed by Plato that eloquence is essential for physicians of the nobility, who are not obedient unless they are first satisfied of the reason, whereas the vulgar can be treated also by incompetent physicians. And innumerable examples verify the observation of Sir William Temple,[67] that, of the three liberal professions, medicine supplies the greatest abundance of materials and the most opportune motives for a varied polite literature. And finally it is to be observed that Pliny is much earlier in time and notoriously erroneous, and rather a malicious than a subtle interpreter of all things.

There is no reliable account of the masters of Asclepiades, and it is not essential, because Reinesius[68] calls him the pupil of an Apollonius, son of Strato. Perhaps it may be said of this Apollonius that he was not the son, but the pupil, of Strato, of whom Galen spoke: but neither of him is any mention as the master of Asclepiades found made in any of the twenty-seven authors. Although he was not, as Galen[69] observes, of a very docile disposition, where his reason did not conduct him, he nevertheless knew how to make use of the discoveries of others; whence there are found the names of seven ancient authors followed in part by him, with improvement of their doctrine in some things where he believed that the truth was more openly revealed to him, from which sprang the accusation of contentiousness which had been given him by the same Galen. It

[67] London author, diplomat, and statesman: A.D. 1628–1699.
[68] Syntagm. Inscr. a cl. XI, P. 4, p. 609.
[69] De Venesectione contra Erasistrateos: tom. IV, p. 3.

can well be believed that the writings of many more had been read
and considered by him, since at his time had already been introduced
for all the luxury of numerous libraries, and precisely the three
centuries which preceded his age were the most enlightened and the
most productive of Greek wisdom.

Of those seven authors, two were philosophers, Heracleides
Ponticus and Epicurus, who flourished more than a hundred years
before him. The former was of the same country of Bithynia, and,
having been born rich, had devoted himself to philosophy for its
sole delight, and had wished to listen to various masters, like the
Pythagoreans, and Plato, and Speusippus, and Aristotle; and had
written many books* on different subjects, and among the others one
on the nature of things and another on the causes of diseases. From
one of these, perhaps, Asclepiades had taken the name of molecules
disconnected or loose, as Sextus[70] and Dionysius Alexandrinus say,
instead of the atoms of Democritus. That in other things also,
however, though not in all, he followed Epicurus, is gathered from
many passages of Galen.

The five other authors were all physicians: Hippocrates, on some
of whose books he commented; Herodicus,[71] who was tutor to the
same Hippocrates, and younger brother of the famous Gorgias,
master of rhetoric at Athens. This physician, many times recommended with praise by Plato, was the first who established medical
gymnastics, separating it from the athletic and the military. Some
of his opinions in respect to the treatment of diseases were examined
by Asclepiades, as may be gathered from Aurelian,[72] who also indicates that he was a sectarian of Herophilus.[73] And from Galen it is
seen that he made great use of his anatomical discoveries. He also
made use of the doctrines of Erasistratus, but by way of improving
or correcting them, since they then constituted the basis of the

* All of these are lost, except one on "Politics" and another entitled "Homeric Allegories."
It is related that Heracleides kept a pet serpent. III, c. 4, p. 136, sec. 318; sec. 32, e. X, p.
686.

[70] Sextus Empiricus: a physician of the first half of the third century A D He was a famous
skeptic, and his two extant works are exposition of skeptic doctrines and a refutation of all
positive philosophy and science. They are a great repository of classic doubts

[71] Herodicus, born at Selymbria in Thrace in the fifth century, 480 B C. His fame has
been eclipsed by that of his most celebrated pupil.

[72] Morb. Chr. III, c. 8, p. 485.

[73] Morb. Acut. II, c. 39, v. 174.

third sect of rationalist physicians, after the Hippocratic and the Herophilean.

He adopted also, as Celsus[74] attests, the precepts of Cleophantus, another ancient physician frequently quoted by Pliny and Galen, who might have been dead about seventy years before Asclepiades was born, and from whose books they say the latter took his idea of constituting one of his most efficacious remedies in the systematic use of wine.

From the good disposition of his body, from the clearness of his mind, from his education, from his doctrine, and also from the sect of philosophy to which he adhered, may be taken a reasonable motive for supposing in Asclepiades both virtue and goodness of mind and innocence of manners.

In the testimonies of the twenty-seven authors who have mentioned him, there is not found made a single reproof of his actions or manners; but, if there are combined the minute and scattered, though imperfect, notices which are given of him, he cannot be denied the praise of having been sagacious, valorous, temperate, truthful, just, and merciful. He showed great discretion in declining, as Pliny[75] relates, the invitations and promises of King Mithridates, not caring for so great wealth.

The private character of that monarch, as is now well known to the world, was that of a man cruel and sanguinary even with the people nearest to him, excessively deceitful and at the same time superstitious and madly credulous in the miracles of drugs: which manners and customs of thought were precisely the most opposite to the nature and wisdom of Asclepiades.

It appears also that Asclepiades was prudent and courageous in not aspiring to the petty and annoying magistracies of his own country, which, as Polybius observes, being of a popular government, through the fault of its citizens, was wont to be full of factions and turbulence. He preferred, after the example of the wise elders, to choose a peaceful voluntary exile, to enjoy, in the condition of a foreigner, the greatest civil liberty and philosophic ease among his books and virtuous assemblies, and natural and critical observations. He showed also the greatest judgment and noble courage in making the city of Rome his permanent residence; which, having then

[74] III, cap 14, p 143, v. 36
[75] H.N. VII, cap 37, P. 37.

already become the capital of the vastest empire, extending through all Europe and part of Asia and of Africa with some form of beneficent government, drew to itself, as Aristides* observed, by land and by sea, everything which in the various seasons had been produced in every country by the labors of the Greeks and of the barbarians; so that whoever found himself in that city could observe the same curiosities of nature and of art as if he had journeyed through all the inhabited regions.

This must have been a very great attraction for a philosopher, besides the marvellous concourse of all the nations, and the frequency of the superb spectacles of the triumphs, and the introduction, which had already occurred, of the Greek arts and sciences among that warlike and magnanimous nation, no longer uncouth and ferocious, but become cultivated and gentle.

It will be impossible, then, to do other than praise the wise resolution of Asclepiades to establish himself at Rome at this time, so opportune for his designs to lead an honest, pleasant, and philosophical life, not participating at all in public discords, but supplying to everyone his advice in the difficulties dependent on the changed condition of the body. His own temperance can be inferred from the perfect health and long life which he enjoyed, and from the high esteem which he had of it in medicine, employing it as one of the most effective instruments of his art.

Besides there being nothing known to the contrary, it could also be argued that he was continent in love from the opinion of Epicurus, who did not believe that love is an instinct or divine influence, like the Platonists, but a weakness of passion, and who said that the wise man does not become infatuated and does not seek unlawful pleasures. In his desire for wealth he showed himself moderate, having learned in the same school that he ought to think of the future and hold poverty in horror as the greatest obstacle to virtue; and that with suitable expenditure cynic filth should be avoided, but that at the same time it is necessary to keep sordid avarice at a distance.

Thus he contented himself with a competent fortune; and although he was highly esteemed in his profession at Rome, yet he was not so intent on gain that sometimes he did not wish to prefer the pleasant

* P. Aelius Aristides Theodorus: A.D 117 to 180. He wrote fifty-five orations *Orations in praise of Rome*, tom. I, p. 100.

oblivion of a solitary life in a suburban villa of his, as Apuleius*
informs us that he did; and so also in this he conforms to the opinion
of Epicurus, who said that the wise man delights in the country.

And by this generous disregard of making money he was able
more easily to resist the insidious promises of Mithridates, which
could not have been other than magnificent. He also fulfilled the
other Epicurean precept, in case of need to seek opportune subsidy
from the same wisdom and genius; whence it does not appear that
he should be blamed, even if, from a motive of interest, as Pliny
would make us believe, he had devoted himself in Rome to the
most honorable and laborious practise of medicine.

Ambition, or the love of glory, came to him equally suggested by
the doctrine of Epicurus, as much as sufficed to defend him from
despite and the outrages† to whch obscure though innocent men
are most exposed in a civil society. And if he was somewhat more
eager for praise, as is imputed to him by Galen,‡ this avidity ought
not to be attributed to his fault, having always been in gentle minds
rather a seed of good and honorable actions.

Nor will it seem that much value ought to be allowed the accusation of pride which comes to him made by the same Galen§ as if he
had rejected the anatomy of Herophilus through vanity, and under-
valued Erasistratus and made no great account of Hippocrates:
since it is well known, by whoever manages matters of study, that
often there occurs disapproval of some saying, even of great men,
without injury being done to their reputation on this account, since
all mortals are equally subject to the sovereign authority of reason.

Caelius Aurelianus seems also to have aggravated him beyond propriety by saying that in his first visits to his patients he cancelled the
medications of other doctors out of spite; since it is more likely that,
on account of his method being different from the usual, not for a
puerile triumph, he sought to satisfy the duty of his profession and of
candor, and freed those who trusted themselves to him from medications which he believed useless or detrimental.

Moreover we encounter many suggestions that he was by his

* Born at Madura in Africa A.D. 130 He wrote a romance, De Asino Aureo, and 4 books
of an anthology: *Florid.* p 362.

† Cf Hamlet: "the slings and arrows of outrageous fortune." III, I, 58.

‡ De Oxymelo a Pisone, tom. II, p. 458.

§ De Usu Partium Corporis, *ragionam.* 6, tom. I, p. 436.

natural inclinations extremely truthful, since it is known from the testimonies of writers and from the fragments of his own works that he had no fear of not concurring in the opinion of others, when his own observations or his reasoning had persuaded him of the contrary. It appears that from this spirit of veracity springs the preference which he gave to the corpuscular and mechanical physics, excluding the poetic suppositions, introduced into medicine, of nature combatting diseases; and thence it was also that he modified the system of the atoms in that which did not appear to correspond with experience.

Of his practical veracity, the greatest argument, as Celsus[76] and Pliny[77] assert, is his having changed in great part the manner of medication, referring all things to their causes, without regard to the authority of ancient abuse. And it is credible that this same natural sense and regard of the truth induced him to manifest it also in the most ordinary actions of his life, as is wont to befall for the most part in philosophers of such fashion; so that he never made any false statements, even in jest, nor employed any deceit for his own interested ends, since there has not remained any indication of this, and since it is seen in the very phraseology of his fragments that he always preferred clear and direct expressions to the dangerous manner of stating the truth under cover of falsehood.

Some wise men reduce almost all the other virtues to veracity, and perhaps justly they believe it the principle and source of all the moral obligations. Certainly with secret force it induces man to precise justice, and instils in his mind that generous honesty whereby he abstains from every fraud and infringement, and rather rejoices in his sincere obedience to the laws of the land in which he lives, because to do otherwise is a continuous exercise of falsehood.

Asclepiades having been thus an ardent friend of truth, it can be believed that he was most just* in all his actions, there not being any indication to the contrary; so much the more that the solemn tenets of his sect[78] are that it is not possible to live happily without being honest, and that, being so, one cannot fail to live happily, and that

---

[76] I, Praefat. p. 3, v. 34.

[77] H.N. XXVI, cap. 3, P. 7, 8.

* Cf. *Hamlet:* III, II, 49–50, "Horatio, thou art e'en as just a man As e'er my conversation coped withal!"

[78] Diog. Laert: X, P. 140, p. 662. Diod. Sic: eclog. XXV, I, tom. 2, p. 509.

the just life is also tranquil, because from injustice spring countless tribulations.

And because the just are also meek and gentle, as Homer[79] said, it should be believed that Asclepiades was very far from offering insults or violence to others, since the rules of his sect[80] also enjoined to calmness, mercy, and benevolence. And if use may be made of a negative reason, his mildness may be inferred from there not being found, among the titles of his many books, any reply, or apology, or defense against any of the innumerable libels which, as Pliny[81] indicates, came out at the appearance of any of his works, and which it is probable that he did not even read and that he despised their enviousness and lack of power to bite, being sufficiently happy in his own sphere and content with his own limited glory, without hating his malicious opponents, and without complaining of their foolish adherents.

But nothing demonstrates his goodness of heart more than the choice which he made of the profession of medicine, in the way in which he understood the function of that art, not as the majority understand it, of preserving health forever unimpaired and of restoring it absolutely when it is lost, but merely of offering the best and most opportune counsel to operate rationally in every occurrence, trying to postpone the apprehended diseases or to alleviate those already incurred, to cure the curable or at least to foresee the outcome of the incurable. In material things, of which one is the living human body, Asclepiades believed, on the reference of Aurelian,* that nothing happens without a cause, and that the causes of events are always mechanical, that is, dependent on matter and motion, and that benefit or harm, although serious and important effects in respect to us, are procedures entirely indifferent in respect to nature, whose objective seemed to him to be the destruction of men no less than their preservation.

With this thought, he believed it humane to have compassion on the afflicted, and it appeared to him that, at least in its intention, medicine is an art wholly beneficent, and reconcilable with perfect innocence. And although from the clearness of his understanding,

[79] Plat. Dial. *Gorg:* tom. I, p. 516. C.
[80] Diog Laert Epicuro X, P. 118, p. 652
[81] H N: XXIII, Cap. I, P. 19, p. 250.
* De Morb. Acut: I, cap. 14, p. 45.

and from his sagacity, and from his power of eloquence, and from his varied learning and his other rare gifts, recognized in him even by his detractors, and especially by Galen,[82] he felt himself suitable to aspire to considerable employments, he preferred to content himself with the dull glory of philosopher and physician.

It has already been admirably demonstrated by Plato, in his gracious dialogue called the Gorgias, that philosophers are by their nature more innocent and more just than tyrants and orators; and by Hippocrates[83] it has been shrewdly observed that all the perfections of the philosopher, both of mind and of manners, are more suitable and also easier for the good physician to acquire than for any others; and with a Homeric phrase, as is often his custom, he adds that the true combination of these two faculties raises man above the rank of mortality.

With this idea, and with the objective of living neither needy, nor despised, nor burdensome, but to be useful to his acquaintances and to do good to all mankind, he devoted himself to the constant and general practise of medicine; and with obvious wisdom he settled in the largest and most populous city which was then in the world and which could therefore supply adequate material for his marvellous ability. And because the old medicine, with the torments of its remedies and the harshness of its prohibitions, seemed to him somewhat inhuman and, as he was wont pleasantly to call it, an apprenticeship or preparation for death, he resolved to reduce it to the mildest terms, freeing it from useless and harmful medications, and substituting for them the judicious regulation and appropriate modification of victuals and of the organic functions.

In the course of perhaps more than fifty years, his principal daily occupations in Rome were of three kinds: first, to treat the sick visited by him throughout the city, and also to give his advice, either orally or in writing, for those absent; second, to give instruction generously to many; and third to write and publish many extremely useful books. Galen grants that he made many cures successfully, and one case in particular showed especially his clinical skill, as Celsus, Pliny, and Apuleius assert.

This was that once, having recognized that a man, whose funeral was being held, was still alive, he resuscitated him and by his counsel

[82] Tom. I, p. 435; Tom. II, p. 458, Tom III, p. 418; Tom. v, p. 341.
[83] De Decoro Medici: sec. I, p. 23, V. 33.

aided him also to continue the enjoyment of life and of health. Celsus describes this episode briefly; and Pliny, who for the most part spoils his narratives with a mixture of the miraculous, reports this as an effect of extraordinary virtue: but Apuleius, in his *Florida*, which are abstracts of notable things from the books which he has read, has preserved for us the circumstances of this account, which render it very credible and ordinary and in fact conformable to that which is known for certain to have happened on other occasions also among us.

He says that Asclepiades, encountering a funeral by chance, recognized signs of life in the man, not at a distance or by vision alone; but, drawing near, he touched him wherever the pulse is most perceptible, and observed attentively the slightest motions of his lips and of his nostrils, since they had put in his mouth the fragrant ointment and had sprinkled all his limbs with perfumes, all which are precisely adapted to the method which also recently has been proposed by a learned French physician* to recognize life suspended and concealed in the longest and profoundist seizures.

In this account is corrected a small error of two very learned men, Conring[84] and Boerhaave,[85] who, to render the thing more credible, changed this man into a hysterical woman, without authority and without need.

The books written by Asclepiades are found so infrequently and so confusedly cited by the ancients that barely can about twenty different titles of his works be found, all pertaining to medicine. Some of them illustrate the first portion of it, which is called physiology, or knowledge of the natural causes of the actions of the living human body in a state of health.

Because Asclepiades, perhaps more than others, considered man, in his bodily operations, subject to physical laws, and thus introduced philosophic theory[86] into the medical art, he esteemed it

* Brubier. *Mémoire sur les enterrements, et dissertation sur les signes de la mort;* Paris, 1749.

[84] Hermann Conring: born at Norden, East Friesland, Nov. 9, 1606; died at Helmstedt, Germany, Dec. 12, 1681: physician, scholar, and author. Introd in med. p. 54, edit. 1654.

[85] Hermann Boerhaave. born at Voorhout, near Leyden, Holland, Dec. 31, 1668; died at Leyden, Sept. 23, 1738: famous Dutch physician, botanist, and chemist. *Praelect. acad. in Proleg. P. 14* "Asclepiades boasted that he had restored from death to life a woman who seems to have been suffering from a hysterical attack." Haller likewise perceived this error. See his notes on this passage.

[86] Haller: addition to Boerhaave *de stud. med.* t. II, p. 303. "Asclepiades either first, or certainly more obviously, founded his practise on theory."

necessary to investigate primarily his minutest components, and wrote a *Book of the Elements*, remembered by Galen,[87] and another of *Respiration and the Pulse*, quoted by the same,[88] these two functions being the foundation of the understanding of life, and of which all the others are either the modes or the effects. In this book, as we gather from Plutarch,[89] Asclepiades made use of the hypothesis, and of the term itself, of atmospheric gravity, which, in the past century, brought such honor to the philosophic school of this city.

By the frequent quotations from Asclepiades about the spirit, which are encountered in many of his twenty-seven witnesses, it appears that it can be conjectured that he had also written about its nature, in so far as concerns medicine, that is considering only its function and its uses, and especially the exercise of the senses. And it appears that thus he had illustrated also the animal functions. And perhaps it was in this book that he expounded that doctrine of his, of which clear traces are found in his fragments, whereby he deduced the origin of human thoughts from sensations alone, rejecting the hypothesis of innate ideas, which have also been excluded forever by the sovereign master of modern metaphysics.*

He treated also of the faculties which are called natural, that is of nutrition and of generation, in another work divided into several books, which he called preparatory; and he wrote considerations on the doctrines of Erasistratus, which were then the most current.

In these books, of which many small fragments are found in Aurelian and Galen, it is seen that Asclepiades had amply explained everything which composes the institutions of medicine and which renders complete the first and most scientific part thereof. But in the same work he laid also the foundations of the second part, more abstruse and more interesting, which consists in knowing the diseases intimately. On this subject he spread himself more, writing one book of *Definitions*, one *Commentary* on some of the short and obscure works of Hippocrates, one treatise on periodic fevers, three on febrile or inflammatory or swift diseases, which are commonly called acute.

---

[87] Gal: *De Elementis*: lib. II, t. I, p. 56, V. 36, 55.

[88] Gal: "Concerning Varieties of the Pulse:" ragion 4, t. 3, p. 51, V. 16.

[89] Plut: *De plac. phil* IV cap. 22, p. 119.

* John Locke: born at Wrington, Somerset, Aug. 29, 1632; died at Oates, High Laver, Essex, Oct. 28, 1704. A celebrated English philosopher, graduated from Christ Church, Oxford, in Feb. 1656; taught Greek and studied medicine there; published "Essay Concerning Human Understanding" in 1690.

He wrote also some books about the Plague, mentioned by Aurelian,* designating by this name not only the dangerous and mortal but also the mild maladies which are produced by some unwonted cause which is common among the inhabitants of that particular region.

He treated besides of some slow or chronic diseases, like the gout, dropsy, haemorrhages, and alopecia, an infirmity in which the hairs fall out from a universal defect of the humors. Galen quotes a long and excellent fragment from him on this malady.

Plutarch, moreover, on the authority of the philosopher Athenodorus,† assures us that it was in the time of Asclepiades that elephantiasis[90] (which is the severe scurvy of the moderns) and hydrophobia first appeared; whence it could be conjectured that either he was the first to observe them or had observed them better than anyone else, and thus had dated the epoch to those two horrible maladies, believed to be new; and that he perhaps was the first to recognize their true and their popularly unknown causes, which are, of the first the corruption of the blood from the prolonged use of improper food, and of the second the venom of a rabid bite. There is found also quoted, by Cassius and by Galen, a book of his on *Ulcers*, which perhaps was a commentary on that of Hippocrates by the same title.

The third part of medicine is the therapeutic which considers the motives resulting from knowledge of the evils, and indicating the changes which ought to be made in the patient's body to abolish them, whence results what is called the method of medication. The majority of authors have combined together the knowledge and the treatment according to the distribution of the kinds of diseases, although some competent masters, and among them Aretaeus,[91]

* Cael Aurel: *Morb Acut:* II, cap. 39, p. 176, num 231.

† A stoic philosopher of Tarsus, surnamed Cananites from Cana in Cilicia, his father's birthplace. He was a pupil of Posidonius at Rhodes, and later taught at Apollonia in Epirus, where Octavius Augustus was one of his disciples He died at the age of 82, and wrote several books not now extant. He told his pupils always to recite the alphabet before saying or doing anything in anger.

[90] Of course we now give the name elephantiasis not to the gross form of scorbutus, which even then was recognized as a dietetic deficiency disease, but to the result of filariasis, or infection with *filaria sanguinis hominis* from the bite of the tse-tse fly.

[91] Aretaeus, one of the most celebrated of the ancient Greek physicians, born in Cappadocia in the first century A.D He wrote in Ionic Greek a general treatise on the causes, symptoms, and treatment of acute and chronic diseases, in eight books, of which all except a few chapters are extant. He was a Pneumatist.

have completely separated the two doctrines; but Asclepiades followed the commoner custom.

The fourth part of medicine treats of the remedies, or, as the ancients better said, of the aids, that is of all those external means or agents which, with the concurrence of the intrinsic vital forces, can produce in the human body modifications conducive either to restoring or to maintaining health.

These aids consist in surgical operations, mechanical procedures, posture, movements, actions, foods, abstinence, and finally in the introduction into the blood-stream of certain substances, in their nature too efficacious and rather harmful, which are drugs or medicines or poisons, according to the primitive and equivalent signification of these three words; and truly they are not beneficial except when they are diluted by the art of the kindly physician.

On this part of medicine there was a book by Asclepiades which he entitled Concerning Common Aids, that is those modifications which man can easily make in his body, and with which he can diminish or remove various infirmities by regulating, with medical means, chiefly five things, as Pliny[92] informs us, that is abstinence from food, wine, walking, and transportation. It appears that Pliny[93] himself, and Sextus,[94] and Aurelian,[95] and Apuleius[96] refer also to a distinct and famous treatise by him on the *Method of giving Wine in Sickness*; and Aurelian[97] quotes one of his on *Enemata*, from which it appears that Celsus[98] has taken nearly all that he says on that subject, naming him as sufficiently conformable to that which to-day is believed to be most reasonable.

The fifth part of medicine is about the methods of preserving health and prolonging life; on which is found mentioned by Celsus,[99] and by Aurelian,[100] and by Galen,[101] a distinguished work of his written to Germinius. In this he condemns purgative medicines, and emetics, and the too artificial exercises of the gymnastic schools,

[92] H N: XXVI, cap. III, P. 7, p. 444.
[93] H N: XIV, cap. VII, P. 9, H.N: XXIII, cap. I, P. 22.
[94] VII, p. 308, Adv. Logicos, num. 91.
[95] *Morb. Acut.* lib. I, c. 15, p 58–59; lib II, c. 29, p. 144.
[96] *Florida*, p. 362, V. 13.
[97] Morb Chron. II and XIII. p. 415, and 184.
[98] II, c. 12, P. concerning alviduction, p. 85
[99] I, c. 3, P. concerning the extensors of the body. p. 29.
[100] *Morb. Acut.* I, c. 15, p. 44; and *Morb. Chron.* II, c. 8, p. 386.
[101] De Sanitate: I and III; tom. IV, p. 225, 246, 247.

and maintained that the best remedy for plethora is abstinence, and praised freedom and variety of life: whence it appears that from him Celsus took the admirable and judicious first chapter of his *Medicine*, and Plutarch the *Discourse against Drugs* in his *Salutary Precepts*. It is likely that of similar subject were also the books sent to King Mithridates, which Pliny[102] says were read at his time.

And it can be believed that he wrote some other books, whose title has been kept quiet, since many of his propositions are found, chiefly in Aurelian and in Galen, which it is not easy to determine whether they belonged to some one of the books mentioned, or to another written by him. So it is not improbable that some of the most praiseworthy doctrines of Celsus, who professed himself his follower, are derived from Asclepiades, although he kept his name quiet. Anciently they did not use exact quotations among scholars; whence it very often occurs that one feels displeasure at their common negligence and often also at the deception of those who delighted to make petty literary thefts.

There remains equally in the dark the knowledge of the relations which he had with his contemporaries. We have already mentioned that Cicero represented him as the esteemed friend of some estimable personages of Rome for dignity and for merit, whose friendship, it is credible, would connect him with others of similar character, composed of learning, worth, and courtesy. Among his friends can be counted also that Geminius to whom he dedicated his books on *Hygiene*, who seems to have been a man of rank, since there are found some of the same family in history and in inscriptions, who enjoyed civil and military honors near those times.

And it appears also that one of his adherents was that Carius Sergius Orata, who lived in the same age, and was a friend, as Cicero[103] attests, of the same Lucius Crassus. This Orata, who is famous in history for the magnificence of his villas and of his aquaria, was the first who made use of hanging baths, as is mentioned by Pliny,[104] by Valerius Maximus,[105] and by Macrobius.* But Pliny

[102] H.N: XXV, cap. II, P. 3, p. 375.

[103] Cicero· De Oratore. I, P. 39, n. 178; De Officiis, III, P. 16, M. 67.

[104] H N. IX, cap. 54, P. 79, p. 359.

[105] Valerius Maximus· A D. 1–50. Roman rhetorician and historian. In 29–32 A.D. he compiled a collection of historical anecdotes De Factis Dictisque Memorabilibus in 9 books, still extant in an abridgement by Julius Paris. Valerius based his work chiefly on Cicero, Livy, Sallust, Varro, and Herodotus.

* Sat. II, 11. Ambrosius Aurelius Theodosius Macrobius, a Roman grammarian of Greek

himself tells us that Asclepiades was the first to introduce their use. It appears credible, therefore, that this ingenious physician invented that manner of making water pleasantly mobile also in domestic baths; and that Orata, being of a practical bent, followed out that thought before anyone else: whence it can be conjectured that he was his acquaintance and friend.

There is found also some trace of his familiarity with the most eminent attorneys of his time in the opinion which he introduced into medicine, as Galen reports, that the human body suffers a continuous dissolution from the particles which transpire from it, so that it can never be said to be exactly the same. Since this opinion, which is otherwise not common, is to be found referred to in one of the fragments of Alfenus,* which the pandects of Justinian have preserved for us, it can be believed that he had received it from his masters, and that by two or three steps only it was derived from Quintus Mucius Scaevola,† the priest, who was the clearest and most authentic interpreter of the Roman Laws, and a great friend and frequent colleague of the same Lucius Crassus, who, as was said, after Cicero, prized himself on the friendship of Asclepiades. So that it is highly credible that Scaevola also esteemed him, and that he had taken from him that physiologic theory of the perpetual mutation of the human body.

Pliny tells us besides that he enjoyed everyone's favor to a marvellous degree; and his expression appears even too strong and exaggerated when he declares that Asclepiades could not have won over to himself almost the whole human race more effectually than if he had come sent by heaven. The fact must be that the medicine of Asclepiades was more reasonable than the usual, and that he, according to the instructions, precepts, and teachings of Epicurus,

---

origin, who lived in the fifth century A.D. He wrote: I. *Saturnaliorum Conviviorum*, VII books of essays and criticism, in imitation of Plato's *Symposium*, and the *Noctes Atticae* of Aulus Gellius. II. *Commentarius ex Cicerone in Somnium Scipionis*, to which we owe the preservation of the Dream of Scipio and Chaucer's "Parlement of Foules " III. *De Differentiis et Societatibus Graeci Latinique Verbi*.

    * Alfenus Varus, born in Cremona, a lawyer, who also carried on the trade of cobbler. Horace refers to him in Sat. I, 3, 130: "Alfenus vafer, omni Abiecto instrumento artis clausaque taberna, Sutor erat.":

> "Skilful Alfenus, throwing all away
> His tools of trade, and shutting up his shop,
> Remained a cobbler still."

    † Quintus Mucius Scaevola: a jurist and orator, who became consul in B.C. 95, and died in B.C. 82. Cicero speaks most highly of him.

was humane and kindly to all, and believed that the injuries which are sustained from others through hatred, or through envy, or through outrage, are compensated by the benefits produced by society itself, and that therefore they ought not to render the wise man afflicted, downcast, and solitary, and that he alone knows how to treat equally well his friends both absent and present, contrary to the custom of the multitude which defrauds or wounds or derides the absent. From the same master he had learned also that friendships are useful, and that therefore they ought to be sought with antecedent and renewed courtesy, as seeds are thrown into the earth; but that for anything more the wise man ought not to count his friends among his permanent and stable possessions, since friendship is a great asset, but in its nature fragile and transitory. With these maxims Asclepiades might be, as he has been represented, universally beloved and at the same time tranquil, if ever at any time any one of his friends abandoned him or through fickleness became his enemy; although there is no record that he ever had enemies of any great importance.

Probably his disciples, followers, and pupils were many, since it is found that the best known physicians who flourished in the three or four generations after him were all of his school. Thus that Alexander Philalethes,* of whom Strabo[106] says that in his time he ruled in Asia a celebrated school of Herophilean physicians, and who was quoted by Galen and Aurelian as an author in high esteem, is known, by means of Theodorus Priscian,[107] to have been a disciple of Asclepiades.

Philonides, a physician of Durazzo, quoted by Scribonius, by Dioscorides and by Galen, is found praised by Herennius Philo and Stephanus† as author of forty-five books and as a scholar of Asclepiades, very much esteemed in that city, which was then very populous and liberal, very near to Italy, where Cicero spent a great part of his brief exile, having been graciously received there.

---

* Alexander Philalethes: an ancient Greek physician of the first century B.C. He succeeded Zeuxis as head of the medical school between Laodicea and Carura in Phrygia.

[106] XII, 580 Strabo B C 54 to A D 24 His geography in 17 books is extant, but his history in 43 books has perished

[107] IV, 315 B edit. Ald Priscian was a physician who lived in the fourth century A.D. in Constantinople. He wrote *De Rebus Medicis* in 4 books.

† Stephanus, a Greek grammarian, resident at Byzantium in the early sixth century A.D., author of *Ethnica*, a geographical dictionary, now extant only in an epitome by Hermolaus, very valuable for its references to ancient writers.

The same Philo mentions in the same place two other scholars of Asclepiades, of whom one was Titus Aufidius,[108] who is cited as such also by Aurelian, and the other, more illustrious, was Nicon of Agrigentum,[109] cited by Celsus[110] and praised by Cicero, in a letter to Trebatius,[111] for the gentleness of his medication, of which he mentions having been able to read a book on *Voracity*, which he had never seen before.

It is credible that that Asclepiadic physician had treated of that infirmity of the stomach which produces a ravenous desire for food, as we know from Aurelian[112] that Asclepiades had treated of it himself and proposed for it a cure, no longer with purgatives and emetics, but with rest and abstinence, and with more suitable selection of foods and beverages. It is probable that Cicero praised him for the gentleness of this method, not because he had proposed the same voracity as a cure for itself, as Rutgers* and other learned critics have wished to explain this passage.

In that same letter of Cicero, mention is made also of Bassus as a physician and friend of his and of Trebatius. This appears to have been that Tullius Bassus[113] whom Dioscorides[114] says to have been of the school of Asclepiades and to have written about herbs. Pliny[115] indicates that he wrote in Greek; and Aurelian[116] quotes a book of his on Hydrophobia, and calls him a friend of Niger. Doubtless he means of Sextus Niger, mentioned among the Asclepiadeans by the same Dioscorides; and it could well be the same Sextus Fabius, scholar of Nicon, from whom Cicero had that book, who had the cognomen of Niger, since from what he says of him it is understood that he was a friend of Bassus.

The others whom Dioscorides calls followers of Asclepiades, and

[108] Titus Aufidius· A Roman jurist, quaestor in B.C. 86, and afterwards a propraetor in Asia.

[109] Nicon Agrigentinus. a Roman physician of the first century B.C. living in Agrigentum, the former Greek Akragas, the modern Italian Girgenti.

[110] Pag. 257, v. 14, MS Printed Micon by error.

[111] Caius Trebatius Testa: a Roman jurist and friend of Cicero, who recommended him to Julius Caesar Horace addressed to Trebatius the first Satire of his second book of Sermones. Cicero's letter was E fam. VII, 20

[112] Morb. Chron: III, cap. 2, p. 436.

* Venusin. lect cap. 21, p. 361.

[113] Tullius Bassus Roman physician of the first century B.C.

[114] Dioscor. Praef.

[115] Lib. I, Autori del lib. XX.

[116] III, cap. 16, p. 233.

who flourished in Rome and knew botany, were Petronius,[117] Diodorus,[118] and Niceratus[119]; and the same Araeus,[120] to whom Dioscorides dedicated his work and who was called an Asclepiadean by Galen:[121] whence it could perhaps be conjectured that Dioscorides himself was of that Sect; and in fact some recipes for external medications, which are found among the fragments of Asclepiades,[122] are found, as if with the same words repeated, in that excellent compiler of medical material, who, though having written in the time of Nero, still saw persisting the credit and merit of the School of Asclepiades.

Certain it is that Scribonius Largus*, who wrote at that same time, bestows the highest praises on Asclepiades, and in one passage calls him his own. And Celsus,[123] who appears to have died in the time of Tiberius, values himself for being his follower, and indeed he followed him even more than he says. And that Cassius, whom Celsus calls the most ingenious physician of his century, shows himself openly an Asclepiadean in the medicinal problems which have remained to us from him, as the most learned Mercurialis[124] also observed, and as such he is recognized by the simple and felicitous cure which he made of a burning fever, as Celsus[125] relates, with cold water alone.

But the most clamorous, noisiest disciple of Asclepiades was Themison[126] of Laodicea in Syria, of whom there are accounts by

[117] Caius Petronius, whom Tacitus called "arbiter elegantiae," lived at Nero's court in the most corrupt days of Rome. He wrote a comic romance, *Satyricon*, parts of which are extant. He died by suicide in 66 A D.

[118] Diodorus Siculus, born at Agyrium, Sicily, was a Greek historian who lived in the first century, B.C., and worked thirty years writing his universal history of the world, in forty books, from the creation to the Gallic Wars, of which nearly half are extant in whole or in part.

[119] Niceratus: a Greek herbalist and writer on plants, one of the followers of Asclepiades of Bithynia.

[120] Araeus: a Stoic philosopher of Alexandria, friend and preceptor of Augustus.

[121] De Compositione Medicamentorum Localium, lib. III, t. II, p. 217.

[122] I. VI, lib. I, tom. II, p. 158.

* 42 B.C. to 54 A.D.

[123] *Composit. medic.* 75, p. 49.

[124] Var. lect. IV, cap. XII, p. 114.

[125] Praef. pag 18, V. 22.

[126] Themison: a celebrated Greek physician, founder of the Sect of Methodici, born and lived at Laodicea in Syria in the first century, B.C. He wrote a number of medical works, of which only a few fragments have survived.

Celsus, Seneca, Pliny, Aurelian, and Galen. They say that after the master's death, he changed the system and established a new Sect, abandoning the search for more obscure causes and observing in the obvious circumstances of maladies the particular conditions common to many, so that he reduced them to a certain few and typical varieties, and gave the name of method to his manner of investigating the manifest and essential resemblances: whence those who followed him were called Methodists. And such were the credit and simplicity of his doctrines that, as Seneca[127] observed, he became the third archimandrite, or head of a Sect, after Hippocrates and Asclepiades, and became heir to his master's glory in Rome, where by chance he came to live after the first years of the Empire.

Certain it is that Augustus had from the beginning for a physician another follower of Asclepiades for leader; this was Marcus Artorius,[128] who was also called Asclepiades by cognomen. And because it is known that the Greek surnames of those who assumed the names of Roman families were for the most part their own original names, it would not be an absurd supposition to imagine that this Artorius Asclepiades might be a descendant from ours.

However it may be about this Artorius, a little less than eighty years ago his antique marble cenotaph with bas-relief and inscription was discovered at Smyrna and was transported to Italy, described and explained by the learned physician and antiquary, Carlo Patino[129]; in which inscription, made in his honor by the Smyrneans, he is called a hero and the physician of the divine Augustus, famous for his vast erudition. Moreover, from the Chronicle of Eusebius[130] it is known that this physician died by submersion in the sea after the victory of Augustus at Actium, which was thirty-one years before our Christian epoch. That Artorius was of the School of Asclepiades is affirmed by Aurelian, who reports some very judicious remarks of his on hydrophobia, on which it seems that he had written a treatise. But he had been rendered

[127] Epist. 95, pag. 599.

[128] Marcus Artorius: a Roman physician, friend of Augustus, whom he attended in his campaign against Brutus and Cassius in 42 B.C. Artorius was drowned at sea after the battle of Actium in 31 B C.

[129] Patav. 1689, 4.

[130] Eusebius Pamphili, father of ecclesiastical history; born at Palestine in 264 A.D.; made Bishop of Caesarea in 315, and died there in 340 A D. He wrote the *Chronicon*, in two books, and many other volumes.

much more famous by the testimonies of the historians Velleius,[131] Valerius,[132] and Plutarch, who attribute to him the merit of having given to the same Augustus, when he found himself with Antonius at the battle of Philippi against Brutus and Cassius, the noble and salutary advice, not to remain in the encampment, even though he was somewhat infirm, but rather to proceed into the combat, like a brave commander; upon which resolution depended his own safety and the victory of that day. And although the historians say that that physician, to persuade him, employed the reason of a dream of his, such a detail is not readily believed; and much less is it subtilized to explain it, as some theologians have seriously done, since it has never been customary for the followers of Asclepiades to rely on similar follies; and it is more probable that Artorius, being old and wise and eloquent, and conversing familiarly and like a friend with the young emperor, had the power to persuade him with the sole, simple, and potent truth of the existing circumstances.

It is supposed by scholars, on the authority of an obscure passage of Pliny, that Antonius Musa* was another famous physician of Augustus, and received distinguished public honors for the cure of him happily made from a slow and dangerous infirmity, happily made at about the fortieth year of his age, as Suetonius[133] and Dion[134] relate.

It appears that it can also be deduced that Musa was an Asclepiadean by his simple method of medication with cold water and lettuce, and by his elegance and varied doctrine, for which he has been praised by Virgil, who was his friend, as also Horace, who shows himself well content with his treatment. And because the Methodici, as Galen[135] observes, had taken their principal doctrines from the

[131] Caius Velleius Paterculus· B C. 19 to A D 31. Wrote a history of Rome.

[132] Valerius Maximus: see previous note 105.

* Antonius Musa· a celebrated Roman physician, born a slave, brother to Euphorbus who was physician to Juba II, King of Mauretania. Antonius was physician to Augustus, and in B.C. 23 cured him of a serious illness (? typhoid fever) by means of cold bathing and cooling drinks Horace alludes to this method of treatment in his Epist. I, 15, 3.

> "My doctor, Antonius Musa, says Baiae
> And its warm baths are not the best for me;
> And that makes me disliked by Baians too
> Since I use cold baths all mid-winter through."

[133] Suetonius· Aug. 59 He wrote biographies of the first twelve Emperors.

[134] Dion Cassius Cocceianus: born in 155 A.D. at Nicaea in Bithynia, son of Cassius Apronianus After an important political career, he retired in 230 A.D. to Nicaea and died there. He wrote a history of Rome in 80 books, of which only the latter part is extant.

[135] Tom. IV, pag. 27.

hypotheses of Asclepiades, it is no wonder if all the Asclepiadeans also appear followers of Themison, like Eudemus, inventor of the cold water enemata, mentioned by Aurelian[136] and by Tacitus, from whom it is known that he was a physician at the court of Drusus, son of Tiberius.

Such also was Thessalus[137] himself, who, in the reign of Nero, had the greatest applause in Rome, as Pliny[138] says, and, in the judgment of Galen,[139] perfected the Methodist Sect, adopting also the theory of Asclepiades. Aurelian mentions, as followers of Asclepiades, a Chrysippus,[140] who wrote about the lumbricord worms of the human body, and a Clodius[141] who sagaciously discovered that the ascarides, another species of worms, are often the material cause of a malady which also corrupts and destroys the mind and the behavior; of which disease perhaps the same Aurelian is the only one who has spoken among all the existing medical writers. Galen* mentions, among the Asclepiadeans, Gallus,[142] Metrodorus,[143] Moschion,[144] and some others, and in general says that at his time the Sect still remained in high reputation.

But already this Sect was extinguished a little after Galen, perhaps because, persisting in excluding everything which was not connected with rigid philosophic truth, it had always two kinds of fairly powerful opponents in medicine, the fraudulent and the gullible: to which was added the universal misfortune by which, through the vicissitudes of great affairs, there prevailed for many centuries in Europe the three grim sisters, slavery, poverty, and ignorance, and exterminated the Greek arts, and especially rational medicine.

But whatever may have been the fate of his writings and of his doctrines, it is evident that much praise has always been given to him by the greater part of those who have spoken of him. No one

[136] Morb Acut. cap. 38, p 171.

[137] Thessalus: born at Tralles, in Lydia, and lived at Rome from A D. 54 to 68 He was buried on the Appian Way.

[138] H.N. XXIX, cap. I, P. 5

[139] Tom. IV, p 77 and 373; and tom. I, p. 27.

[140] Morb. Chron. IV, cap. 8, p 537. The works of Chrysippus in 705 books, B C 280-207, are not now extant.

[141] Clodius Macer. Chron. cap. 9, p. 545, a physician and Roman governor of Africa in 68 A.D.

* Tom. I, pag 94.

[142] Carus Cornelius Gallus: B C. 66 to 26: a Roman poet, physician, and politician.

[143] Metrodorus of Stratonice in Caria: a physician who flourished about 110 A.D.

[144] Moschion: a Greek physician, author of a work on gynaecology in the second century A.D.

disputes with him the honor of having been one of the few principal institutors of the art of medicine, and in this supposition those also reason about him who show themselves less favorable, like Aurelian and Galen.[145] But some more distinctly, like Apuleius,[146] have called him chief of all other physicians, except Hippocrates alone.

And by the philosopher Antiochus[147] he was called second to none in medicine and skilled in philosophy; and by Celsus[148] he was esteemed a good authority to be followed in many things; and by Scribonius[149] a very great authority; and by Marcellus[150] a most excellent physician; and by Strabo[151] memorable for his doctrine; and by Cassiodorus[152] most erudite; and by Cicero[153] eloquent; and by Pliny[154] wise and of marvellous persuasiveness; and by Galen[155] an accurate, polite and powerful reasoner.

By the extinction of ancient literature, which followed about the sixth and seventh centuries after Christ, when the greater part of the Greek and Latin books were lost, until the sixteenth century, the fame of Asclepiades lay obscure and silent.

The first of the moderns who then revived Greek medicine, among whom not the least praise is due to our predecessors in the Tuscan School, were predominantly followers of the opinions of Galen; wherefore, since he had been, as has been said, somewhat harsh and unjust towards Asclepiades, it is no wonder if they allowed themselves to be prepossessed against him, and if they believed without further investigation in the accusations of Pliny and of Aurelian: insomuch that Eustachius,[156] otherwise very scholarly, incautiously

[145] Celsus praef. p. 4 and elsewhere. Seneca, epist. 95. Pliny: H N. XXVI, c. 3, and often elsewhere. Sextus Empiricus, p. 412 and p. 493. Galen: Tom IV. p. 372; Tom. V, p. 397. Aurelian passim.

[146] Florid: p. 362.

[147] Sext. Emp. lib. VII, p. 412.

[148] IV, c. 4. Ulceration of the fauces (diphtheria)

[149] Epist. 3.

[150] Cap. 14.

[151] Lib. XII, p. 566.

[152] Tom. II, 509.

[153] De Orat., I, 62.

[154] H N. XXVI, c. 3, P. 7.

[155] Tom. I, p. 435; II, p. 458; V, p. 345.

[156] Bartolommeo Eustachio: 1500 to 1574 A.D. Professor of Medicine at Rome from 1562. One of the great modern anatomists, first to discover the heart-valve which bears his name, and the stapes, and first to describe accurately the auditory tubes and the thoracic duct. *Libellus de multitudine* cap. 16, Ven. 1566. pag. 136.

allowed himself to be carried away, when he called him unworthy of the name of philosopher and of physician for not having thought like Galen. Moreover Mercuralis[157] and Alpinus[158] began to take some account of his opinions; and Sassonia[159] deigned to call him the most humane of all the physicians who have ever been in the world.

But in the last part of the seventeenth century, which seems to have been the most scientific of all the other centuries of which we have memorial, reason became more powerful than authority, and not only many very important new discoveries were made, but many of the opinions of the ancient sages, whose writings had been lost, were found plausible and true, which had been represented as absurd by intervening writers. Thus were revived Philolaic[160] Astronomy and the Democritan Physiology, which were the first steps to rise to even greater height; and in therapeutic medicine the Asclepiadean simplicity and prudence and sagacity regained vigor, whence derived the purest and best modern Tuscan medicine chiefly through the industry of the immortal Redi,[161] who, in the selection of his simple, pleasant, and safe remedies, confesses to have been guided in his first youth by the example of Asclepiades, which he encountered while reading the work of Celsus.[162]

At the same time also those two clear lights of the distinguished Neapolitan School, Tommaso Cornelio and Leonardo di Capua, perceived the excellence of the doctrines of Asclepiades. Cornelio praised the corrections which Asclepiades made in a method too complex, as it was inconvenient and dangerous; and Capoa deserved the praise of having been the first to revive the authority of the opinions of Asclepiades himself, explaining openly and more fully than the others the agreement of some of them with reason.

In this current eighteenth century several scholarly men have

[157] See note 124.

[158] cfo Horace: Sat. I, 10, 30. "Turgidus Alpinus jugulat dum Memnona."

[159] De phoenigmis, Patav. 1593, pag. 5.

[160] Philolaus: native of Croton, contemporary of Socrates, instructor of Simmias at Thebes, where he lived. He wrote a work on Pythagorean philosophy, on which Plato based his dialogue of Timaeus.

[161] Francesco Redi: born at Arezzo, Italy, on Feb. 18, 1626; died at Pisa on March 1, 1698. An eminent Italian naturalist who wrote a book "Experiments in the Reproduction of Insects," 1698.

[162] Lettera 13 in Tom. IV, pag. 44.

spoken of Asclepiades, like Ammannus[163] in his notes to Aurelian, confessing that the greater part of the Asclepiadean reasonings are the same as those of modern philosophers; and Daniel Le Clerc[164] fairly fully in his *History of Medicine*; and Barchusen in his dissertations on the origins and progress of the same; and Garofalus[165] in his explanation of his antique bust; and finally Albert Haller[166] in his *Additions to the Method of Medical Study by Boerhaave.*

But, without lacking in the respect due to men of such deep learning, it can be observed generally that these and other illustrious moderns either have simply repeated the statement of some one of the twenty-seven ancients, or, treating of Asclepiades, have believed, without investigation, in the invidious judgments of two or three of them, or have neglected the most important details, or through erroneous interpretation of some obscure passages, or for some other cause, have, without authority, attributed to him sentiments which he did not have, absurd and contary to his own system.*

[163] Johann Konrad Ammannus· born at Schaffhausen, Switzerland, in 1669; died at Warmond, near Leyden, in 1728; teacher and writer on deaf-mutism. Author of Surdus loquens, 1672, De Loquela, 1700, notes on Aurelian, 1709.

[164] Daniel Le Clerc· French physician, author of *Histoire de la Médecine*: Amsterdam, 1702

[165] Benvenuto Tisio Garofalo. 1481 to 1559 A.D. Born near Ferrara Pupil of Baldini.

[166] Albrecht von Haller: born at Bern on 16 Oct. 1708, died there on 12 Dec., 1777 Celebrated Swiss anatomist, botanist, and physician

* There is seen, for example, Boerhaave, who, in P. 14 of his Praelectiones, speaking of Asclepiades, has erred thrice. first in making him later than Aretaeus; second in saying that he boasted of certain secrets through his long life; and third when he boasted of having resuscitated a hysterical lady. And finally Haller himself, in his Supplement to Boerhaave, *De stud. med* , Tom. I, p. 304, says that "Asclepiades praised the magic cures purchased in Rome and the superstitious medicines."

Fragments from Asclepiades of Bithynia.

Arranged and Edited by
CHRISTIAN GOTTLIEB GUMPERT,
Doctor of Medicine and of Surgery.

Preface by
CHRISTIAN GODFREY GRUNER.

Weimar, 1794

Published at the expense of the
new bookstore, commonly called
INDUSTRY COUNTER.

DEDICATION

To the most Illustrious and Reverend
ANDREW HUMPHREY WIERSBINSKI,
Abbot of the Monastery of Bledso,
of the Sacred Cistercian Order,
Most Pious Knight of the
*Order of Saint Stanislas.**

Likewise to the most Noble and Excellent
SIR BOGUSLAS MAXIMILIAN BOIANOWSKI.

And to my most Worthy Patrons and Subscribers
Who deserve to be cultivated with
the Utmost Respect.

This Little Book
is dedicated
by
The Author.

---

* Bishop of Cracow and Patron Saint of Poland: born 1030; killed 1079 A.D,

Do not wonder because you perceive your most worthy names in the front of this book. Such are your kindnesses to me that I count myself thrice and four times fortunate on account of this occasion whereby it befalls me to be so happy as publicly to bear witness of my pious and grateful disposition towards you. Immense indeed are the services which have been well and excellently rendered by you to me.

Would that I might reveal to you all my feeling, whereby you might at length realize by how many great names I am bound to you. But lest all the advantages which have accrued to me from your good will towards me should seem to perish completely with an ingrate, I have dared publicly to declare here my disposition most indebted to you. Furthermore, there is nothing more in my wishes than that you should continue to employ hereafter towards me the favor of which you have always held me worthy. May the fates ever be kind to you!

Most observant of your names,
Christian Gottlieb Gumpert.

Preface to Readers

I have often wondered at the negligence of our scholars in pursuing the study of medical history, and at their audacity in disapproving the writings of hundreds of others maintaining this argument, as if, forsooth, without this knowledge, the art itself could be well established or anyone could be, and be regarded as, a great physician. For in the monuments of the ancients, both the greater and the more recent, there are the seeds and principles of manifold and various doctrine, and it is very important to know what and how much they have written about medical affairs, what decrees and precepts they have left consigned to their successors, either for imitation, or for condemnation, or for restraint.

In estimating these rightly, with an accurate and trained judgment, it is necessary that you should not be diverted in the opposite direction, nor devote either too little or nothing to study, or everything to gain, and nothing to humanity, amenity, and refreshment of spirit. Hence I cannot but smile at the solicitude of certain judges who are both dangerous and repeatedly write on a book, *unless what you are doing is useful, your fame is vain*. This indeed I praise in itself, and approve, so far as it pertains to laborers, but condemn and disapprove, if it concerns a scholar. Poverty pleases no one, unless he affects it, however great we assume him who prefers to be richer than others, wiser, more learned, than to be content with broken furniture, and says he prefers to be so than to be hungry.

But it is of little value to measure the knowledge of the mind by utility alone, since, in appraising it, one man is wont and ought to adopt one way, another another. Each employs his own measure, and praises only what he himself has taught or done. But in the end that seems to me to be useful which benefits medicine, and pleases readers, and makes for the advancement of knowledge. Other things pertain to chance, and have no effect for either increasing or diminishing utility.

Very recently certain physicians, whom I name for honor's

sake,—Ackermann,* Metzger, Sprengel,†—have resuscitated, as if from the lower world, the literary history of medicine, despised and rashly neglected for some time past, and by their example have instigated others to return to former centuries, to unite the old with the new, and devote some time to the history of the art.

Although this does not produce a doctor, nevertheless it adorns him, frees him from the prejudice of novelty, moderates his judgment, and justifies him to all the centuries. Hence I conceive a good hope, if I hear that a beginner is comparing our scholars with their predecessors, is reading many things, but prudently and much. For he, when maturely he questions history, and suffers himself necessarily to be enrolled among the scholars of history, will not fail himself or science, and, imbued with a distinguished discipline, prepared in style and eloquence for the medical art, will apply his apprenticeship rightly, will seek a little glory in the first specimen of learning produced, and will lay aside this love of letters only with life itself.

There remain in ancient, medieval, and more recent history many things in which the diligence of those who dare can expatiate farther, many things abandoned and uncultivated which it can cultivate more copiously, many obscure things to which this is to bring light. To undertake these things and bring the affair to a conclusion is true praise and worthy of a young man. Such things the author of this book has dared, when he undertook to outline the life, sayings, and writings of Asclepiades of Bithynia, by far the most famous physician of his age. Nor, as far as I see, has the outcome failed the attempt, since he has come well prepared and instructed for writing history.

He knows medicine, both old and new, therefore he could judge of Asclepiades from his own level. He knows the sources whence he ought to derive the motives of narration, hence he has disregarded the turbid streams in which, if you except some of the recent, there is hardly what you desire. Moreover he examined the writers of the

* Johann Christian Gottlieb Ackermann: born February 17, 1756; died at Altdorf, Bavaria, March 9, 1801. Author of "Institutiones Historiae Medicinae" (1792), and biographies of Hippocrates, Theophrastus, Dioscorides, Aretaeus, Rufus of Ephesus, and Galen.

† Kurt Sprengel: born at Boldekow, near Anklam, Prussia, August 3, 1766; died at Halle, March 15, 1833. Professor of Medicine, from 1789, at the University of Halle. Author of "Versuch einer pragmatischen Geschichte der Arzneikunde," (1795.).

later age, of whom there was an abundance, but with the result that he gave first place to the ancients, Celsus, Caelius Aurelianus,* Galen, and second to the more recent, some of whom expressly took care to describe Asclepiades, like Antonius Cocchius[1] and Bianchini;[2] others more carefully gave the history of his life and teachings, like Clericus[3] and Barchusen;[4] others generally found written what they had found said by others, but not truly or correctly enough.

Finally the narrator of Asclepiades, in this undertaking, was not so familiar with the trivial or the commonplace that he left untouched or unexplored anything which he thought was in his field, but carefully, learnedly, widely, and copiously reviewed the things which should express his perfect likeness. Thus the author availed many and will please the majority, who lack the leisure and intelligence for sedulous investigation, but not the curiosity. With such a work, if I am not wholly mistaken, he will be looking ahead to his own reputation; since he who first ventures to produce such things, bids us expect even greater and more distinguished ones. I therefore gladly and gratefully invoke the utmost favors for this worthy, modest, and excellently trained young man.

Jena, Saxony.   CHRISTIAN GODFREY GRUNER.
7 January, 1794.

* Born at Sicca, in Numidia, where he lived during the second century of the Christian Era. His writings, belonging to the Methodic Sect, are I. Acutarum Celerum Passionum, 3 books; Paris, 1533 and 1826. II. Chronicarum Tardarum Passionum, 5 books; Basle, 1529 and 1566. III. Medicinales Responsiones: a comprehensive treatise on medical science in the form of a dialogue, published in 1871 by Val Rose in his Anecdota Graeca et Graeco-Latina, Vol. II.

[1] Discors. sopra Asclepiade, Fior. 1764.
[2] La Medicina d'Asclepiada, Venez. 1769.
[3] Hist. de Medec. P. II. 3 p.
[4] Hist. med. Diol. XII, p. 248.

Chapter I

VARIOUS OTHER MEN, DESIGNATED BY THE NAME OF ASCLEPIADES, WHO OCCUR IN THE WRITINGS OF THE ANCIENTS

P. 1.   It is established among all that from Aesculapius, that renowned evil-averting deity of remotest antiquity, first his own family, then, when, on account of the increase of his divine cult, and the many temples constructed to him, his own offspring no longer sufficed to perpetuate duly his sacred rites, those outside the family also were ascribed to a society who, for the purpose of soliciting aid, assisted the sick in celebrating the temples, the entire order of priests received the name of Asclepiades. As time advanced, this name was proper to all those who were bound by oath to the schools which flourished in the name and authority of Aesculapius, chiefly at Cnidus and at Cos. But there is no discussion here about all these.

Rather we take in a later age certain men, skilled in our art and designated by the same name, who, connected with Aesculapius by no bond of descent or college of priests, either referred to their ancestors that name received by heredity, or had vindicated it for themselves by many excellent works in the art, in investigating whose history we ought to delay briefly. Doubtless, while we have the disposition, we ought to inquire a little more accurately into the history and doctrine of that Asclepiades, an illustrious and ingenious physician among the Romans who not only first made Greek medicine hateful to the severer descendants of Romulus, but also, cultivated by its own merit, made it more pleasing and acceptable to all.

Before we proceed to discussing our subject, we may speak about those other men who have been distinguished by the name of Asclepiades, lest perchance we should confuse the celebrated deeds of someone else by the same name with those of our Bithynian, and thence be prevented from being able to judge rightly.[1]

---

[1] Examples show that this has already been done. So Le Clerc, Hist. de la Méd. II, III, 10, relates that Lionardo di Capua, "Raggion," p. 367, considered our Bithynian to be one and the same with Pharmacion.

But before we proceed further, it will help to remember that many things which pertain to the history of those men may be read already treated by Reinesius,[2] Walsh,[3] Sponius,[4] Fabricius,[5] Le Clerc,[6] and others, whom we shall mention in our text itself. It is our duty, therefore, to collect here those details which are found touched upon in those writings and to exhibit a complete cycle of Asclepiades; but especially to take care lest perchance those errors which have crept into the writings of those men distinguished by sufficiently great learning should be repeated here anew.

P. 2. *Asclepiades Pharmacion*

The line is led by a certain Asclepiades, known as Pharmacion, so-called on account of the drugs, to whose description, composition, and method of exhibition he devoted a special work.[7] He seems to have lived in the times of Nero or of Domitian, as Garofalo and, following his opinion, Walsh[8] attempt to prove.

His pharmaceutical books are named by Galen in his own writings concerning the composition of medicine according to places and kinds: doubtless he had written ten books about drugs, of which the first five described external medications and bore the name of Marcella on the title-page; the other five later ones described internal medicines, and owed their denomination to a certain Mnason.[9] Le

---

[2] In notes for inscriptions, and in letters to Rupert and Hoffmann.

[3] In "Selected Medical Antiquities."

[4] "Recherches curieuses d'Antiquité."

[5] Bibliothec. Gr. To. XIII, p. 90 sqq.

[6] Hist. de la Méd. II, III, 10. p. 417.

[7] Gal. de composit. medic. sec gen lib I To. II. p. 525. edit. Basil. Asclepiades, called Pharmacion, wrote ten books besides adding those about wild beasts and women; and he himself gave the announcement of drugs; and of many he gave also the preparation, and of some also the manner of their use.

[8] Garofalo, Giornal. de' Letter d'Ital. 1712. T. II. (Le Clerc II. 3. 9 p. 413), and Walsh, in antiq medic. select. I. 1 , believed that this can be gathered therefrom, because Galen reports (de compos. medic sec loc. II. 2. To. II p 180) that a drug, which Asclepiades had described in his books, had already been employed by a certain Charicles a distinguished doctor in the age of Tiberius. But if, by this method of investigation, the age of this Asclepiades ought to be established beyond all doubt, with greater likelihood, rather with certainty, we can maintain, according to the same Galen, that he lived after Andromachus, after Dioscorides and Scribonius Largus. Galen de compos medic. sec loc. VII. To. II p 263 VIII. To II. p. 280 et 284. X. To II p 309. sec. gen. VII. To II. p. 409 Vid. Rhod. ad Scribon. Larg P. 7.

[9] Galen, de composit. medic. sec. gen. I. To. II. p. 325. He himself wrote about them (the external) first Marcella; and second, third, fourth, and fifth Mnason. The works of this

Clerc undeservedly ascribed to him the pronomen of Marcus Terentius.[10]

L. Arruntius Sempronianus Asclepiades

P. 3.   The memory of this man is consigned to oblivion on a stone, found on the Via Nomentana and deciphered by Reinesius, whose inscription is "To L. Arruntius Sempronianus Asclepiades, Physician of the Emperor Domitian."

C. Calpurnius Asclepiades

P. 4.   Among other Asclepiades, Caius Calpurnius is particularly prominent as a renowned physician in the times of Trajan, whose memory a distinguished monument of antiquity thus perpetuates: "Caius Calpurnius Asclepiades,[11] a Physician from Prusa at Olympus, obtained for his parents and himself and his brothers seven states from the divine Trajan. He was born at Cos, March 5, in the thirteenth year of Domitian."

From this monument we can gather how greatly he was esteemed by the most honorable men of his age. For on the same marble we read: "Approved for his learning and character by the most distinguished men, he sat among the magistrates of the Roman people. He was presented by Trajan with the rights of seven states."[12]

Caius Calpurnius was born 840 A.U.C. 88 P.C.N., and died in the seventieth year of his age, 910 P.U.C., in the reign of Antoninus

Asclepiades were collected by Fabricius Bibl. Gr. To. XIII. p. 91. sqq. add. Walsh. l.c. and whom Reinesius praises there in his letter to Rupert. ep. 36.

[10] We cannot omit here the error committed by Le Clerc l.c. He says namely that this Asclepiades was celebrated by the pronomen of Marcus Terentius, relying on the passage of Galen, de composit. medic. sec gen. VII. p. 410. But if we inspect that passage a little more accurately, we shall learn that Galen is here describing the poultices which Pharmacion had reviewed in his books, and from them taking the poultice of Marcus Terentius Asclepiades (so say edd. Basl. et Charter). It is clear, therefore, that this Marcus Terentius is either a later man distinguished by the name of Asclepiades or that instead of Asclepiades should be read Asclepiadeus (from the sect of our Bithynian), which greatly amuses me, since from that passage of Galen we have ascertained that the poultice produced by Marcus Terentius ought to be ascribed to our Bithynian, Asclepiades.

[11] Walsh. in antiq. med. select. l c. besides Reinesius and Sponius, where this marble is read, praises also Almelov. ad Strab p. 860. Lamp de honor. privil. et jurib. medicor. p. 110. et Vinck, amoenit philol. medic. p. 169.

[12] Walsh has already refuted Sponius, Le Clerc, and others, who were convinced as if Trajan had given the seven states themselves to Calpurnius, and demonstrates admirably that this is to be understood only of the rights of the seven states.

Pius. Since he took his origin from Prusa, Reinesius (*not. ad inscript. p. 608.*) Sponius, (*recherch. curieus. d'ant. p. 431.*) and Walsh, adding pebbles to their opinion, had persuaded themselves that he was not only a citizen of our Prusa but also a native and the heir of the art and perhaps the grandson of Calpurnius. But they are greatly in error. For although he was a citizen and a native, nevertheless he could not be a grandson, since between Calpurnius and him of Bithynia there intervened a space of almost two hundred years, as Le Clerc well observes (II,3,10,420.).

P. 5.   *Asclepiades Philophysicus*

Galen mentions a certain other physician, designated by the name of Asclepiades, who, that he may be differentiated from others, is called *philophysicus*, from his study of natural history. Apart from certain medicines, which Galen describes, there is nothing further noteworthy about him.[13] By others he is erroneously called philosophicus instead of philophysicus, and from this perverse reading Rhodius and Scrib. Larg. (p. 237) were doubtless deceived, and thought that this Asclepiades philophysicus was in no way different from the physician and philosopher of Prusa; this Le Clerc has already refuted. Altogether it seems more satisfactory to read Philophysicus, which both the Charterian edition and the circumstance itself suggests, since this name pertains more to a druggist than that sought from the study of philosophy.

P. 6.   *T. Aelius Asclepiades*

To a certain ancient stone which we find deciphered in Grote (p. 335, 1), excavated near the Amphitheatre at Rome, we owe the memory of this physician. From it we have learned about a certain freedman of Augustus, whom thus the stone portrays: T. Aelius Asclepiades, physician and surgeon of the morning game.[14]

P. 7.   *P. Numitorius Asclepiades*

Walsh, from a stone deciphered by Grote, as also by Humphrey Panuvinius and Scipio Masseus, brings forward Publius Numitorius

[13] Galen, de composit. medicam sec. loc. VII. To. II. p. 271. et lib VIII. To. II. P. 283.
[14] Besides Walsh in antiq. medic. select., where he speaks of this Asclepiades, whom he there praises, Lipsium. Saturn. I. p. 909. vid. Mercurial. de art. gymnast. lib. I.C. 12. p. 96. distinguished by the people of Verona, for honors formerly enjoyed.

Asclepiades, a freedman of Publius, an ophthalmologist, and esteemed among the people of Verona for the honors which he formerly enjoyed.

P. 8.   *L. Scribonius Asclepiades*

It may be questioned whether some other physician ought to be reckoned in this assemblage of Asclepiades, who, like others also whose history we have already outlined or intend to outline, owes the accepted memory of his name to an inscription which is as follows: L. Scribonius dedicated this stone to his sweet wife Scribonia. Rhodius surmises that this Scribonius Asclepiades was Scribonius Largus himself.[15]

P. 9.   *Asclepiades Titiensis*

Caelius Aurelianus (*III, Morb. acut. 5, 55*) brings forward another Asclepiades, whom he calls Titiensis. Le Clerc doubts whether he ought to be differentiated from other physicians distinguished by the name of Asclepiades, or, instead of Titiensis, wishes to call him Citiensis, that is the Citian. Nothing further is known about him.

P. 10.   *Asclepiades the Son of Apollonius*

The memory of this man comes to us from a stone excavated at Smyrna, which Fabricius (*Bibl. Gr. TXIII. lib. 6, p. 90*) describes from Reinesius (*XI, 5, p. 610.*) as a cube standing upright on one angle, in which is sculptured a toga-clad statue on the right, and on the left a square gravestone, on which is placed the head of a hunch-backed old man, and standing underneath a boy; at the right of the statue a pile of volumes. On the upper edge of the stone are read these words: "To Asclepiades the son of Apollonius and Artemidorus," and in the midst of these words a wreath on which is carved: "Forsaken."

P. 11.   *Asclepiades the Ephesian*

Here finally the line closes, concerning whom the same Fabricius offers this inscription from Fulvius Ursinus p. (98.)

> "Dear to his friends and of doctors the best,
> In sacred childhood he was blest;
> This tomb his memory doth maintain:
> His spirit it can not contain!"

---

[15] vid. Rhod. ad Scribon. Largum.

To Phonteius Phortis Asclepiades[16] of the Ephesian race, laboring under fifty years, ten months, twenty days, and fifteen hours, Briseis of Egnatia, his wife, for the sake of remembrance.

P. 12.   *Should Arius be numbered in this assemblage of Asclepiades?*

Le Clerc wishes also to include in the number of Asclepiades a certain Arius Asclepiades, supporting his opinion on the authority of Galen, whose references, however, where he speaks of him, he neglects to cite. Therefore with all possible diligence I have looked through the works of Galen, where I might find what pertains to him. There I have found that Galen makes mention of a certain Arius who was an Ascelpiades, or of the sect of Asclepiades of Bithynia; but he is not distinguished[17] by the name of Asclepiades.

P. 13.   *Does Gallus Marcus Belong Here?*

Nor can we be less uncertain about Gallus Marcus, whom Le Clerc has rashly allowed to obtain a place, like that Arius, among the other Asclepiades. It all goes back to the passage of Galen, (*de composit. medic. sec. loc. VIII To II. p. 283.*) where he makes mention of Gallus Marcus the Asclepiades. So read the Basil. and Charter. editions. But we think that an error lies concealed here. To what end the article "the" before Asclepiades? What? if we read Gallus Marcus the Asclepiades? (*as in de. compos. med. sec. gen. V. To II. p. 392.*) Arius the Asclepiades. From these, therefore, which we have especially stated, we gather that Le Clerc was deceived in this, and we cannot agree with him when he declares that, besides Asclepiades the Bithynian, Galen makes mention of four others of the same denomination, when rather, besides the Bithynian, so far as we know, no other occurs except Pharmacion and Philophysicus: and the passage of Galen (*de compos. med. sec. loc. VI. To. II P. 252*) where the discussion is of two Asclepiades who wrote about the composition of drugs, and is not to be understood about Pharmacion and Arius, as Le Clerc falsely surmises, but about Pharmacion and Philophysicus.

[16] Le Clerc thinks this Phonteius Phortis ought to be removed from the number of Asclepiades because he declares of himself that he derives his descent from Aesculapius and his offspring; but from the inscription itself nothing of the same appears.

[17] Galen, de composit medic. sec. loc IV. To. II. p. 217 Arius Asclepiades V. To II. p. 226. sec gen V. To II p. 392. sec. loc. VIII To II p. 283 mention is made of Arius Asclepiades; but since in all other passages of Galen he appears as Arius Asclepiadeus, even in this place we think Asclepiadeus ought to be read for Asclepiades.

P. 14.   *Asclepiades Myrleanus*

Well, this is the entire cycle of Asclepiades who, though physicians, were willing to render eternal with their names the memory
of the chief physician, Aesculapius, which, before we gird ourselves
for our main work, we have thought it worth while to compose in
order that thence the Bithynian Asclepiades may emerge more
intact. We doubt not that among writers of antiquarian history,
and in collections of monuments, stones, and coins, other physicians
rejoicing in the same name, but hitherto unknown, may lie concealed. But these which we have collected are sufficient for our
purpose. Now nothing further remains than that we should briefly
delay for Asclepiades Myrleanus, who perhaps gave Pliny[18] cause
to speak falsely of the Bithynian. He lived in the times of Pompey
the Great, and taught the art of grammar at Rome. (See concerning
him *Fabric. ad. Sext. Empiric. advers. Gramm. I, 2. p. 225* and in
Bibl. Gr. Vol. II. p. 54.). Other men, who, though not physicians,
nevertheless were distinguished by the name of Asclepiades, and of
whom Garofalo edited a catalogue (*Giornal de' Letter. d'Ital.
1712. T. II. Le Clerc p. 413*) we clearly omit here, because they
contribute nothing to our subject.

[18] vid. infr. cap. II. P. 20.

Chapter II

ASCLEPIADES THE BITHYNIAN

P. 15.   *Introduction*

Having explained what required to be said first, let us pass now to the subject itself, which is our dear concern. According to the manner and custom of all who recount the lives of distinguished men, we shall begin with those things which pertain to the origin and family of our Bithynian. But it is surprising how few things which illustrate his life have come through to our times, as if submerged in the writings of the ancients; and those few, how disarticulate and mutilated, how depraved and obscured by fictitious imaginations of the mind! Not only more recent writers who have cared nothing what they put into print about Asclepiades, but some among the ancients themselves, like Pliny,[19] have not cared what they wrote.

Among more recent writers, some have seemed to think it worth while if, for the sake of interest and pleasure, they should beguile time for readers, and adorn his history with well devised details.[20]

Others have neglected this in order that they might differentiate from him various others distinguished by the name of Asclepiades.[21]

Whence it has resulted that some things are mixed together which ought to be separated, and others separated which ought to be combined. It is our function therefore to put together the few things which remain to us, to distinguish the true from the false, to reject comments, to separate rash mixtures and altogether so to conduct ourselves that Asclepiades shall emerge intact, neither depraved nor undeservedly adorned.

P. 16.   *Native Land of Asclepiades*

As far as concerns his native land, the ancients have reported that he was born in the city of Bithynia which is called Prusa.[22]

---

[19] vid. infra P. 20.

[20] As from Anton. Cocchi Discors. I. on Asclepiades Bianchini reports La Medicina d'Asclepiade. Discors. I. P. VIII cf. supra praefat.

[21] Vid. supra cap. I. P. I. not. a et P. 5 not. n.

[22] In the writings of the ancients three cities occur of the same name. First of these is

Whence it has resulted that he does not always occur in the writings of the ancients merely by the name of Bithynian or Prusan,[23] by which he could be more easily distinguished from others. But with the author of the medical introduction, intruded into the writings of Galen and falsely ascribed to him, there occurs another name by which Asclepiades is distinguished; namely here he is called Cianus: Asclepiades the Bithynian, who is also called Cianos and Prusan. (*Gal. T. IV. p. 372.*).

P. 17.   *Can Asclepiades Be Called Cianus?*

Concerning Asclepiades Cianus[24] very great contention has arisen among learned scholars. Nowhere among the ancients does Asclepiades occur adorned by this name, except in that passage of the introduction: and if we inspect the words themselves a little more accurately, they are found disarticulate, corrupt, and depraved: whence it has resulted that learned scholars have diverged into different opinions.

Le Clerc, (*Hist. de la Med. II. 3. 12, p. 133. in edit. prim. Amst. 1702*), trying to display a remedy for that mutilated passage, instead of Cinus prefers to read ἐκεῖνος, "he". A sufficiently ingeniously devised conjecture. To be sure the author of the introduction names there the chiefs of the sects; and of the rational sect: Hippocrates, Diocles, Praxagoras, Herophilus, Erasistratus, and Mnesitheus: then follows Asclepiades the Bithynian, who is also called Prusan. But Le Clerc brings forward another conjecture besides that men-

---

Prusias so-called in the most ancient times from the river Cius washing it, as is clear from Apollon. Rhod Argoa.

> "So then they raught Cianis' sacred land
> On Arganthonius mount, by Cius washed "

Cius is a river meandering through Mysia Vid Plin H N V. 40 Apollod confirms that Cius is a city of Mysia Biblioth I C 9 P 50 cf Heyne in not ad Apollod. p. 185 sq Salmas. exercit. Plin. ad Solin. p 877 Stephan Byzant. S.V. Kíos. Both the other cities are of Bithynia and are called Prusa, of which one was founded by Hannibal at the foot of Olympus, the other is situated at the foot of Mount Hypius, as Pliny testifies, H N V. 43 Garofalo has commented more fully concerning these three cities (Le Clerc p. 411).

[23] Asclepiades the Bithynian Sext Empiric pyrrh hypotyp III 9 f. 36 p 136 Strabo XII p. 849. edit Almel. Frag in Gr chir. libr. e collect. Nicet edit. Cocchi p. 154. To Asclepiades the physician from Bithynia Galen de Theriac ad Pison. T. II p. 418, and the same in many places Prusiensis Plin H.N. VII 37.

[24] Lionardo di Capua Raggion I imagines that Asclepiades and Cianus are different men, and he ascribes Cianus to those other chiefs of sects who are named in that passage: vid. Le Clerc. Hist. de la Med. II, 3, 9

tioned. For perhaps, says he, if the word ἐκεῖνος were superfluous, and not used in this sense by writers, it could be eliminated from the context.

Galen in his writings always calls him simply Asclepiades, or bestows on him the name of Bithynian, or denotes him in some other way; since in those times Asclepiades had not yet escaped from the memory of men, still thriving as the chief founder at that age of the Methodic sect. But excepting Galen, at the time when the blind and almost divine prestige of Galen had almost completely destroyed all memory of older physicians,[25] it was necessary that the author of the Introduction should denote Asclepiades by these names, in order that he might more quickly recall the memory of that most ancient Asclepiades, and thence beware that he should not be confounded with other men of the same name, who both had lived and were still living, or with any author who wished any doctrine of his to be manifested in this way.

P. 18.   *Journeys of Asclepiades*

Concerning the natal year of Asclepiades, his parents, his boyhood and youth, his education, institutions, and teachers, the way in which he went through the work of learning, nothing is known to us.[26] This only we have ascertained: that he went to Parium,[27] journeyed through the Hellespont, and stayed at Athens.

In what places he professed his Art, he has collected many ob-

[25] This appears evidently from those medical collections prepared by the order of emperors for the sake of itinerary use, as Bernard well observes to Theophan, Nonnus. (in introduction not. i.) now first published, as they say, as a posthumous work, adorned with an immense appeal of erudition Here belong the collections of Oribasius, Aetius, and others, who were already persuaded they had done enough, if, with blind zeal, they should bring out and prepare all Galen's immense volumes or the works of other medical coevals, taking no account of the celebrated ancient physicians, whose excellent works in those times were almost completely consigned to oblivion: whence it also resulted that the elegantly written works of our Asclepiades completely perished, which Cocchius with so sad a heart notes (ad script chir. Gr. a collect. Nicet. p. 154).

[26] Bianchini relates (la medicina d'Asclep. disc. I. P V. II vid supra praefat) how beautifully Ant. Cocch. (disc. sopra Asclepiade) has adorned this part of the story Walsh, in antiquit. medic select. I.1, reports that the ancients mention Asclepiades as the pupil of Apollonius the Erasistratean But among the sectarians of Erasistratus, I have known no other Apollonius than him, who bore the name of Memphis Vid. Col Aurel III chr morb 8 P. 101 et IV chr. morb. 8 P. 114 But nowhere in the writings of the ancients do I find him or any other Apollonius mentioned as a teacher of Asclepiades hence plainly I do not know from what source Walsh has derived.

[27] Famous town of Mysia. Vid Plin. H N. V. 22f. 40 et VII, 2, f, 2.

servations pertinent to this, some of which have been handed down by Cael. Aurel. (*II, morb. acut. 22. P. 129.*)

Then he betook himself to Rome where, until extreme old age and death, he practised his art adorned with immense praise and rejoicing in good success, as we will demonstrate in many ways.

P. 19.   *Concerning the Age When he Came to Rome*

But the distinguished name and reputation, which he bore above all others, he obtained first when he took up practise among the Romans. The age itself, in which he came to Rome, and flourished there, and met his end, is not yet so clear that it can be computed to the minutest moment of time. The difficulties in which the whole thing is involved derive from two passages of Pliny and of Cicero, of whom the former (*H.N. XXVI, 3*) refers Asclepiades to the age of Pompey the Great, but the latter (*de orator. I. 14*) to that of Crassus the celebrated orator: whence it has resulted that those also who have written anything about Asclepiades walk different ways. Some, led by the authority of Pliny alone, like Ackermann (*inst. hist. med. p. 235*) think him coeval with Pompey: others, like Walsh, invoking Cicero as a witness, (*in antiq. med. select. l.c.*) have persuaded themselves that Cicero himself used Asclepiades as a physician and friend. Others add no pebbles of opinion to either, and from this latter group stand out Cocchi (*ad. script. chir. Gr. p. 154*) and Bianchini (*la medic d'Ascl. P. 5 et 7*). To be sure these men declare that Cicero pretended that that confabulation was held between men endowed with the greatest wisdom and all dignity, A.U.C. DCLXII, in which Lucius Marcius Philippus and Sextus Julius Caesar were consuls, and M. Livius Drusus tribune of the people; so that that famous evidence about Asclepiades seems attributable not to Cicero himself but to an older man Crassus, who died a few days after that confabulation was held; as Cicero himself relates (*de Orator III. ab init*). Cocchi then continues in these words: "Since those words of Crassus perhaps indicate that Asclepiades had then finished his life (*Plin. H.N. VII. 37*), it scarcely is credible that he was an intimate with either Cicero or Pompey, who were then still boys.

"And so not altogether rightly does Pliny seem to have referred Asclepiades to the age of Pompey the Great, perhaps deceived by this, because he saw some books of his inscribed to Mithridates, a king whom he knew to have been conquered by Pompey."

In the same way judges Bianchini, who moreover adds: "at the time of Pompey the Great: that is to say, under his consulship, or in the greater apogee of his fortunes."

But I frankly confess that I recede a little from the opinion of these men. For even if it is true, according to that Ciceronian passage, that Asclepiades belongs to the age of Crassus,[28] who used him as a physician and friend, nevertheless it does not follow thence that he had already met his end at the times of Cicero and Pompey.

From all these things, enough and more than enough light seems to emerge to make it clear that Asclepiades is to be assigned to the age of Crassus and Cicero, which seems already to have been done by *Sprengel (Vers. einer pragm. Gesch. der Arzneik. I. 1. p. 436)*; although it cannot be denied that Asclepiades was beginning to reach old age, while Cicero and Pompey were rejoicing in the years of their youth.

But therefore it is not possible for a definite opinion to be established concerning the year, either when Asclepiades reached Rome or when he met his fate: nevertheless this is established, that he spent his life there in the seventh century of the city, mostly in the earlier part of this century.[29]

P. 20. *Refutation of Pliny's Statement that Asclepiades Taught Rhetoric at Rome*

There has obtained, and still obtains among various men, who have treated the affairs of Asclepiades, an error whereby a large amount of splendor and adornment is detracted from him. Hence

---

[28] Perhaps we may be doubtful whether these words rightly refer to Crassus. Doubtless we know that Cicero only assumed that Crassus and Antonius were conferring; but actually he put his own opinions into the speech of Crassus, as he put those of his brother Quintus into that of Antonius.

[29] We cannot arrive at a clear and certain computation of the years, which is already proved enough and more than enough by the difference which exists between the various reckonings of writers. So Anton. Cocchi. (disc. I. sopr. Asclep) imagines that the year in which Asclepiades was born corresponds to A.U C. DLXXX. A.C.N. CLXXIV, as Bianchini relates (la medic. d'Asclep. disc. I. P. VIII). *Ackerman*, in chronologic consideration ad. inst. hist. medic. p. 585. ad annum U.C.D.C.L.A.C.N.C. considers that Asclepiades met his fate about this time. Vid. *Bianconi* epist. de Cels. aetat. p. 141.—Sprengel, on the contrary, maintains that he came to Rome about this time.

nothing ought to be more precious to us than that we should refute Pliny, who first gave occasion for that error, and the men who have followed his words. Doubtless Pliny (*H.N. XXVI. 3. f. 7.*) speaks thus:—

"Antiquity lasted secure and will vindicate the great remains of an established order, until Asclepiades, master of oratory in the age of Pompey the Great, not having made enough money in the art, suddenly turned to other things than the forum, of intellectual interest: and, (as was necessary, for a man who had neither done this nor known the remedies to be perceived by the eyes and by experience) flattering with burning and meditated daily oratory, renounced everything." If these statements had been true, then it is obvious how greatly the merits of Asclepiades diminish.[30]

But it's a good thing Pliny was deceived in some way! For we know now (P. 18) that Asclepiades, before he came to Rome, had professed medicine in the Hellespont, at Parium, and at Athens, and there had made various original observations pertaining to medicine. And if the ancients had not informed us about this affair, all his teaching would prove sufficiently and more that it could not happen that from a rhetorician, plainly imbued with no previous disciplines of medical art, should suddenly emerge, as if aided by the arts of Proteus, so upright a physician, skilful and beloved by all.

It is therefore placed beyond all controversy that Pliny here speaks so falsely of Asclepiades that immediately at the first glance the contrary strikes his vision. But when the question arises in what way it could happen that Pliny should err in a matter which is not far distant from his times, it seems very likely to us that he did not sufficiently distinguish our Bithynian from that Myrlean, (*Cap. I. P. 14. Cf. Conring. de hermet. medic. C. 9*) a famous Grammarian among the Romans in the age of Pompey the Great, and this affair became confused with those of the former; or that he did not sufficiently examine the history of our Prusan himself. For this is altogether true, that Asclepiades excelled above others in eloquence, which that very Plineian passage itself bears witness, in which his fervid and meditated oratory is praised. But especially

---

[30] Le Clerc (Hist. de la Méd. II 3, 4) and Ackerm. (instit. hist. medic P. 186. p. 135), alone with Pliny invoking faith in this thing, fell into the same error, which Bianchini was the first zealously to refute (la medic. d'Asclep. disc. I, P. VII).

the distinguished words of Crassus in Cicero (*de orator, I. 14.*)[31] Nay Galen, though he always tries to depreciate the merits of Asclepiades, nevertheless in many places praises his eloquence or his oration adorned with ingenious art.[32]

Therefore it could have happened that Asclepiades, when he came to Rome, had not yet found out how brave a physician, about to engage in practise, would be before he would prefer to act the part of a man forsaken and eloquent, whereby perhaps he might win the gratitude of Romans primarily favorable to this discipline of letters, and thence might bring it about that in practising his art thereafter he might be exposed to fewer hindrances and inconveniences. Brave, no doubt, because Archagathus had died not long before, and he had not been able to ignore the hatred which inflamed the Romans, too severe upon him at first, who acquiesced with a persistent mind in the commonness of death and in the institutions of their ancestors.

But when gradually they became known to the Romans, and they were so carried away by his perfect discourse and art that they perceived plainly that the medicine which he professed was plainly different from that of Archagathus, and best suited to the Roman mind: and when the failing severity of the Romans began wholly to vacillate more and more, so that at length they understood that the disciplines of the Greeks are a great reward and delight: then Asclepiades began to practise medicine with good courage and unexpected success. But he was not suddenly made a physician from a rhetorician, who learned no remedies and was imbued with no doctrines of the art: so that rather he came to Rome already as an experienced physician.

P. 21.   *Testimonials of Asclepiades*

Since these things were so, not long afterwards he attained his greatest glory and splendor at Rome, not only on account of his medicine and philosophy, best suited to the mind of the Romans, but also on account of the eloquence and prudence with which he tried to render his companionship welcome and beloved by all.

---

[31] Cic: "Nor did Asclepiades, whom we have used as a physician and friend, surpass other physicians with eloquence, surpass in this because he spoke ornamentally, but used the function of medicine, not of eloquence"

[32] Galen. de naturalıb. facult. I. 19. TI 4 9 p' contr. ea quae a Juliano in Hipp. aph. etc. c. 5. and in many other places.

This is proved more than amply by the testimonials which occur in great number among writers. Pertinent to this primarily are those words of Crassus of which we made mention in a preceding paragraph.

Strabo (*XII. p. 849. edit. Almelov.*) counts him among the worthiest Bithynian men in respect to education. Apuleius (*florid. p. 362. edit. Elmenh.*) says that he was chief among others, among the famous of physicians, if Hippocrates alone be excepted. By Antiochus Academicus (*in Sext. Empiric. adv. Log. I.f. 201. p. 214.*) he is called "second to none in the medical world, and also touching philosophy." Celsus esteems him highly, and calls him the good author of many things which he himself had achieved.

Scribonius Largus, in a letter to Callistius, calls him the great author of medicine, and makes many words against his detractors. It is doubtful whether the praise with which Marcellus (*de medicam. c. 14*) distinguishes Asclepiades pertains to our man. Dioscorides (*lib. I. praefat.*) praises him and his sectarians most highly. Galen (*de natural facult. I.T.I. 17 p. 97.*) although not always accustomed to slander the merits of Asclepiades, cannot deny him praise. The sect instituted and named by him also increases greatly the fame which he enjoys, which for a long space of time has obtained the height of glory. Hereafter there will be talk about it by many.

P. 22.   *He Declines the Promises of Mithridates*

But what chiefly makes the name of Asclepiades famous, and witnesses that it was also distinguished among foreigners, is that Mithridates, that celebrated and literate king of Bithynia, no less learned in medical art, who with immense promises tried to solicit his learned native to leave Rome, and by his arrival, said he would increase the number of learned men, with whom he was daily crowded.

But Asclepiades, beloved and made much of by the Romans, joined with chief men of every dignity, spurned those envoys and promises, and declined to leave Rome. For him Asclepiades had composed some volumes, which, solicited by the city, he sent before him as precepts.[33]

----

[33] vid. Plin. H.N. XXV. 3. and VII. 37.

P. 23.   *Death of Asclepiades*

Asclepiades continued his life at Rome until extreme old age, with the highest praise, deserving well of all who had impaired health, made much of by his coevals, rejoicing in that singular good fortune that through his whole life he was afflicted by no disease, and did not meet his end by the dissolution of bodily disease, but by a fall down stairs. Hereupon Pliny raves equally falsely and ridiculously (*H.N. VII, 37*), "by a pledge made with fortune, no doctor would be believed if ever he had been sick himself; and victor in extreme old age died by a fall down stairs."[34]

[34] Fabric. Bibl Gr. T. XIII p. 87. praises Longwilliam Harcuauctum in hist. microbiol. (Mem de Trevoux A 1718. Octbr. p. 630) narrating that Asclepiades, a Prusan physician, would be still alive without a fall which ended his days at 150 years (Ant Cocchi contends that he lived about eighty years and died A.U.C. DCLXII. in the CSS. M. Philippo et Sexto. Julio. Caesare.)

Chapter III

The Writings of Asclepiades[35]

Common Aids.[36]*

Bald-Headedness.[37]

A Book about Respiration and the Pulses.[38]

Enemata.[39]

Ulcers.[40]

Periodic Fevers.[41]

Book about Terms.[42]

About the More Obscure Books of Hippocrates.[43]

The Duties of Doctors.[44]

Aphorisms of Hippocrates.[45]

Concerning Dropsy.[46]

Concerning Cardiac Lues.[47]

Volumes for Mithridates sending his Precepts from Rome.[48]

Books Against Erasistratus About Preparations.[49]

Three Books About Rapid or Acute Diseases.[50]

About Pulses.[51]

Books of Greeting to Germinius.[52]

---

[35] Cf. Fabric. Bibl. Gr. P. XIII p 90. Bianchini. La medina d'Asclepiade disc. I.P. IV.

[36] Cael. Aurel. lib. I. acut. C. 15 p. 59. lib. II. chron. C. 13. p. 417.

* This denoted what we mean by "First Aid."

[37] Galen. de comp. medic f. 1. lib I. p. 167. To. II.

[38] Galen. de differ. puls. lib. IV. p 61. T. III.

[39] Cael Aurel. lib. II, chron. C. 15. p. 415.

[40] Cassius Quaest. med. probl. XXXX.

[41] Cael. Aurel lib II. acut. C. 10. p. 96.

[42] Seems to be the same with the books which he wrote of definitions Cael. Aurel lib. I. acut.

[43] Galen. Comment. I. in Hippocr de offic. med. T.V. P. 665.

[44] Galen. Comment. I in Hippocr. de offic. med. T.V. P. 667, 674.

[45] Cael Aurel. lib. III. acut. C. I. p. 181.

[46] Cael Aurel. lib. III. chron. C. 8. p. 478 and 489.

[47] Cael. Aurel lib II. acut. C. 39. p. 176.

[48] Plin. H N. XXV. 3.

[49] Cael. Aurel. lib. II. chron C. XIII. p. 416 Scrib. Larg. in praefat. p. 16.

[50] Cael. Aurel lib. I. acut. p. 2. lib. I. acut. C. 15 II 45. and very often in the whole work.

[51] Galen. T. III. p. 51. de differ. puls. lib. IV, unless it is the same as that which we have mentioned above.

[52] Cael. Aurel. chron. C. 7. p. 386.

Safeguarding the Health.[53]
About Elements.[54]
The Administration of Wine.[55]

[53] Cels. I, 3, p. 29.
[54] Galen. de element. lib. I. P. 56.
[55] Cael. Aurel. lib. II. acut. C. 29. p. 144. Sext. Empiric. adv. Logic. I, f. 91. p. 338.

Chapter IV

THE STATE OF ROMAN AFFAIRS BEFORE AND ABOUT THE AGE OF ASCLEPIADES

P. 25.   *State of Public and Civil Affairs*

When we survey at a single glance the state of Roman affairs, what it was at the close of the sixth and beginning of the seventh century of the city, no one can fail to be overwhelmed with supreme joy, noting how the Roman state has raught a distinguished peak of power and splendor, having relied on such scanty and feeble supports at the outset, so that now it seems to hold the hegemony and empire of almost the whole circuit of the world. Nevertheless, so many things, which were brought forward as reasons for the Roman republic, now have been destroyed and are noted as special causes why sooner or later that mighty mass would fall in its own ruin; so that soon after the war with Hannibal was finished,[56] Philippus,[57] Antiochus,[58] Aetoles,[59] and Galates were conquered[60] and yielded to the power of the Romans. The legions, which long had joined hands in luxury, softness, and effeminacy with these peoples rolling in abundance of riches, brought back to Rome not only their immense resources but also their utterly depraved customs. What wonder that the Roman state soon was found destitute of the virtues of its ancestors. After Perseus was finally conquered,[61] after Corinth and Carthage[62] were destroyed, the descent from virtue, the transition to vice was not gradual but by a precipitate course. The old discipline was deserted, new discipline introduced, the state was turned from vigilance into sleep, from arms to pleasures, from business to idleness.

Luxury, pleasure, softness, effeminacy, banquets, tables distinguished with all delights for the palate, revelling, commerce with

[56] A U.C. 552.
[57] A U.C. 557.
[58] A.U.C. 562.
[59] A.U.C. 565.
[60] A.U.C. 566.
[61] A.U.C. 586.
[62] A.U.C. 608.

harlots and wantons, and an amazing number of documents pertaining to obscene life seem to replace the daily, honorable ways of living. An immense number of servants brought into the city from the conquered provinces upsets all the uprightness of morals remaining to the Romans, and completely depraves the adolescent youth with Greek arts and tricks.

P. 26.   *The State of Literature of this Age*

It is established among all, that the intelligence of the Romans, although in the age which we have chiefly described, it had greatly declined from that characteristic of their ancestors, nevertheless now for the first time had become suitable for cultivating letters and humane studies. Before this time very few rudiments of Roman genius are extant. The mind, as if roused from a profound sleep, suddenly throws off the defences and chains which hitherto have kept it sound and firm, though rude and untrained, and bestows upon literature all the strength which it possesses. Men not nourished in letters migrate from Greece to Rome, and there scatter the seeds which soon bloom forth with a notable luxuriance and abundance of fruit.

P. 27.   *The State of Philosophy*

But what first concerns the cult of philosophy among the Romans, it is known that a great space of time had elapsed before they said what they thought about it: and writers, relating the fortunes which philosophy had experienced among the Romans, begin from that distinguished legation of Athenians, at the end of the sixth century, at which time they sent philosophers as envoys: Carneades the Academic; Diogenes the Stoic; and Critolaus the Peripatetic. It is said that the Roman youths were so carried away by the discourse and eloquence, that with their whole mind and enthusiasm they embraced the doctrine of wisdom; and neither the authority of Cato, nor decrees of the senate against rhetoricians, promulgated not so long afterwards, nor other safeguards of this nature, with which the more severe and austere Romans strove to check the advance of wisdom, could bring it about that the love of philosophy, which had already struck such deep roots, should be completely extinguished. At the outset of the seventh century let us rather assume distinguished men holding foremost positions in the republic, so inflamed with love of philosophy that their returns from the administration of public affairs alone pertained thereto.

As an example of all, it is permissible to name here Scipio Africanus and Lucullus, of whom the latter, a pupil of Antiochus of Ascalon, a coeval of Asclepiades the Bithynian, by means of an immense collection of books, which at his expense had been hidden away in a gallery, greatly spread abroad the study of philosophy. About this time, therefore, we note that at Rome already the *Porch* and the *Academy* were renowned, and there were not lacking those addicted to syncretism.

But as for what pertains to the doctrine of Epicurus, it seems that Asclepiades must be judged among the first who transplanted it to Rome. It is known that the discipline of morals instituted by some of his sectarians in Greece had been so far defamed and contaminated that it passed into contempt of almost all: and it is no wonder that the Romans, who, although it might be gathered from their mode of living, had adjusted a very distorted doctrine of Epicurus concerning pleasure to their kind of existence, from the not yet fully extinct severer temperament of their ancestors affected and aspired to an austere philosophy of Epicurus with as much affection as the Stoic and other schools. Nevertheless also among distinguished Romans there were not lacking those who were wholly involved in this kind of philosophy. As an example of all in this exceptional age, we mention Atticus and Lucretius. But coeval with our Asclepiades seem to have been Torquatus, Velleius, Titus Albutius, and perhaps also others, a catalogue of whom is edited by Gassendi (*de vit. et. morib. Epic. lib. II c. 6*).

The State of Medicine

P. 28.   In the more ancient times of the republic there was no medical art other than what exists among all uncultivated peoples; nor did the lack of it incapacitate the Romans, who rejoiced in supreme good health strengthened by military service and the labors of agriculture. But from the description of this age (P. 25) we saw that things had so changed that the Romans ought to demand the practise of medicine as supremely necessary. The firm and robust organization of their bodies had so far deteriorated from depravity of morals, from precious ointments brought to Rome from foreign countries,[63] from soft garments and coverings, from relations with harlots and pederasty completely sapping the vigor of life,[64] from tables adorned with luxurious supplies of viands,[65] from nocturnal feasts celebrated under the pretext of sacred rites, and from other such depraved things destroying all humanity,[66] that in no other way, except by the aid of medicine, could its solution be met.

But since the art of Aesculapius was almost the last of the Greek disciplines which the Romans subsequently cultivated at Rome; it is not remarkable that the Romans, before the true salutary doctrine became familiar to them, employed, as masseurs and medicine-men, servants imported from Greece. Finally in the year of the city DXXXV, Archagathus first came to Rome as a physician; and from the benevolence which he received, it is permissible to infer what and how great was his necessity from the Romans. Moreover the ill-will with which the Romans were inflamed against the Greek physicians, and which he himself had increased, as is said, by his cruel method of treatment, had not yet fully escaped the memory of men; whence it resulted that the art of Archagathus soon passed into the contempt of almost all.

P. 29.   *Conclusions from these things which we have related thus far*

Now Asclepiades arrived, and turned the eyes of all upon him as if sent down from heaven. From the outline of the age at which it is probable that he came to Rome, it appears clearer than noonday that he arrived at a time most favorable for him and for his art. Aided by external circumstances, he himself turned them admirably to his own advantage, a thing which may be gathered from the whole book. On account of the doctrine of Epicurus,[67] upon which he had built his own, he was equally dear to many who thought as he did, and to almost all on account of the practise of his art and his other

---

[63] Plin. H N. XIII 1–5 Scip apud Gellium N.A VII, 10

[64] Gell N.A XIII, 23 Polyb. II 1457. ed. Gr. Macrob. Saturn. II, 10

[65] Polyb. II 1459 edit. Gron. Gell N A II. 14.

[66] Liv lib XXXIX (c 8–18)

[67] Sprengel Versuch einer pragmat Gesch der Arzneik. T. I. p. 456.

"Herein also lay an artistic concept of Asclepiades to make precisely such a system as foundation of his own theoretic doctrine that employed no transcendental or intellectual principles for explanation of the modifications of the animal body, but explained everything from the immediate operations of physical forces, and therefore was perfectly made for a nation which neither loved nor was accustomed to the exertions of the spirit."

virtues, which captured the popular favor in all from whom the hatred which had entered the rest of the mind of the Romans had completely dissipated.

I can add no pebbles to this opinion. For assuredly he is to be despised by all, who in order to look out for his own better fortune and investigative life, adjusts his whole doctrine to any mind of men. Least does it seem that Asclepiades ought to be marked for this disgrace, who, on account of the doctrine of Epicurus, was first subjected by him to medical disciplines, and deserved well of the art. Then when we have ascertained that he had already devoted work to the practise of his art in his native land, it is no doubt likely that at that time he had already established a system when he had not yet thought that he should some time go to offer the Romans the aid of medicine.

Then from the description of the fortune which philosophy under-went among the Romans (P. 17) it may be seen that there were only a very few among them who gave words to the doctrine of Epicurus. And at the climax, from these and many others who altogether esteemed all occupation of letters, Asclepiades became of great im-portance on account of the system in which he had outlined medical science. But patients, demanding his aid, doubtless cared not at all whether he was bound to any other system of philosophy.

Chapter V

PRINCIPLES OF THE PHILOSOPHY
INCLUDING ATOMS

P. 30.   *Introduction*

When we return to the first origins of the doctrine which treats things divine and human, we observe that the human mind, before it could think for itself, acquired the power of producing all things which strike the senses for knowledge of matter alone: then, when we inquire into the disciplines of the old philosophers, we can easily elicit that this is certain and approved to their mind, that the origin of those things from nothing was plainly not comprehended or perceived in mind. The concept of matter was first outlined by those philosophers by whom the Ionic School is composed, especially cultivated by reasons of Pythagoras, and finally refined with the more subtle genius of the later Eclectics to the point of detailed ingenuity.

No doubt Xenophanes and Parmenides reached the point of proving matter continuous, with no empty space, as we call it, intervening: whence it resulted that they denied all motion, origin and destruction of things. Leucippus[68] was the first to take offense at their doctrine, which is contrary to all experience, and proposed and suggested that matter is divided into the most minute particles; by which means he adjusted it to the nature of things and to experience. Democritus, and, in the following age, Epicurus, attempted to support with new arguments the doctrine which now it is our purpose to describe.

P. 31.   *Atoms and Empty Space*

To the philosophers who have especially performed the work for this discipline of wisdom, it was equally beyond all doubt with the philosophers of all antiquity that "nothing ever developes divinely from nothing," whence it results that those atoms, which contain in themselves the origin of all things, persist eternally.[69] To these atoms

---

[68] Aristotle has admirably expounded this whole subject de generat. et corrupt. I, 8, p. 395, 96., and the whole passage there is worthy to be perused in full.

[69] Aristot. de Coelo I.7.T.I. p. 345. ed. Casaub. Diogen. Laert. lib. IX.

and to empty space, also equally eternal, all things which we perceive owe their origin: and there is no third substance stated beyond those two named elements of bodies.[70] Nature, in which the atoms rejoice, is one and the same for all.[71] They are infinitely minute, and, since they are not susceptible to sensation, can be conceived only by the mind.[72]

They are indivisible:[73] for it is not possible for a body to be infinitely divided. They are solid,[74] as bodies opposed to empty space: they are infinite in number, as empty space can be bounded by no limits: hence it is also obvious that the universe is infinite in every direction.[75] Of all other things which we call sensible there are experiences of qualities, although sensible things are composed of these.[76] But to affections of those elements pertains form, of which there is required an infinite variety,[77] in order that thence there may be the more easily explained the origin of so many and such various and diverse things which strike the senses. Besides these various forms, they differ among themselves in accordance with the relation and position which they obtain in reference to one another in concrete objects.[78]

Besides those atoms, elements of things, Epicurus seems to have implied certain other substances which are neither atoms, properly so-called, nor bodies which meet the senses in the nature of things, composed and compounded of corpuscles; they themselves compose bodies perceptible to the senses.[79]

[70] Aristot. de Coel. I.7.T I. p. 345. Galen. de element. I. p. 46. T.I. Lucret. de rer. natur. I V. 430–483.

[71] Aristot. de Coel. I.7 T I 345. Cicero de fin. I. 6.

[72] Aristot. de generat. et corrupt I. 8. p. 396. Galen I. 1. Lucret. IV. 265–329.

[73] Aristot. de generat. et corrupt. lib. I.T I p. 384. Galen. l.c. Cf. Epicur. epistol. ad Herodot. apud Giog Laert. lib X Lucret. I.V. 528 sqq.

[74] Cic. Acad quaest. IV. 37 Diog Laert. IX, 30 31. Lucret. I.V. 483–635.

[75] Lucret. I.V. 919 sqq. Aristot. de gener. it corrupt I 8 T.I. P. 396.

[76] Aristot. de gener. et corrupt. I 1.T I. p. 384 Sext. Empir Pyrrhon hypotyp. III, 4. f. 33. p 137. idem. adv. Phys II. f 318. p. 686. Galen I.1. Lucret. II. v. 729. sqq.

[77] Aristot. de gener. et corr. I 1 T I p. 384. Cic. de Nat. Deor. I 24. Hence in Sext. Empiric. adv Phys. 1 c Lucret. II. V. 333 sqq.

[78] Aristot. Met. I.4 T.II. p. 645 "For Leucippus and Democritus say that being differs only in rhythm, and position, and manner. And of these, rhythm has form, and position has order, and manner has position."

[79] Ackerman instit. hist. med p. 133. primarily urges this distinction between atoms, concretions, and bodies, as the system of Asclepiades explains. Hence it is necessary that we should pause briefly in explaining this matter. Ackerman relies on a passage in Diog Laert. X. f. 42. epist. ad Herod. "The atoms are bodies from which combinations arise and into

P. 32.   *Motion of Atoms*

Motion pertains to the disturbances of atoms, and when one and the same nature is in them all, the motion itself is one and the same, not diverse, wandering, or incoördinate.[80] There are atoms which are as eternal as the empty space through which they pass: hence also motion itself is eternal, and not arising from any origin.[81] But since atoms are simple according to their own nature, perfectly solid, and indivisible, and cannot undergo any so-called internal change, they can rejoice in no other motion, except what takes place in respect of the various atoms, (change from place to place).

P. 33.   *Origin of Perceptible Things*

But that motion of the atoms is the cause of origin of all things which we perceive. They combine, and by this combination is formed the nature of all things. Doubtless those atoms, with such an infinite quantity of forms diverse from one another, constitute an infinite force for the infinite variety of combinations which they can undergo.[82] Therefore the origin is the combination of atoms, as

---

which they dissolve." There occur to me two passages from Lucretius which seem to demonstrate the same thing.

Lucret. I.484 sqq.

> "Bodies are partly elements of things,
> Partly the plan from which their nature springs."

Lucret. II 132 sqq.

> "Prime movers are the elements of things,
> Then those which briefly are in bodies formed,
> And as if next the nearest force that springs,
> Driven by their blind blows from the low ground
> Themselves arise as if on sightless wings."

[80] Arist de Coel. I 7 T.I. p. 345. Leucippus and Democritus say that the nature of them is one; and, as we say, it is necessary that their motion is the same Philosophers differ about the manner and norm in which the atoms move Vid Cic de finib I.6. de fat. 12. Plut. de placit. philos I 25. Galen de elem I p. 47. T I Lucret. II v. 60 sqq

[81] Galen de Elem I.T I. p 47. Lucret II V. 294 sqq Aristot Phys. VIII. 2.T.I p. 327.

[82] Galen de elem I. P. 47. T I. "Either they combine somehow with one another, or approach and recede and separate and combine again with one another in accordance with such associations And from these and other combinations, everything is made, even our bodies.

Diog. Laert IX. 31 Lucret. II 864 sqq V. 1018.

> "In matter, as in things themselves, there are
> Intervals, paths, connections, weights, and blows,
> Assembly, motion, order, place, and forms,
> When they are changed, of course things must change too."

Aristot. de gen. et corrupt. I 8.T.I. p. 396.

their separation is their destruction: and change is changed position and relation.[83] But since neither power nor quality is inherent in atoms, it is inevitable that they should owe their origin to combination of these.[84]

P. 34.   *The Rational Faculty. Fate*

Since it was understood and approved in the mind of philosophers that, except for atoms and empty space, nothing is as eternal as those elements; it is clearer than light that they could not have thought anything about the eternal mind, by which the nature of things was either formed or effected. And it was not necessary that they should anxiously adjust a power of this sort to their doctrine, which stood well established and constructed with this object. For by eternal and inviolable law, all things are so prepared that they can proceed in this and no other way. By law and by nature atoms are solid, indivisible, infinitely minute; by law they are provided with manifold forms; by law they move through empty space; by law finally they come together and constitute a nature of things that is perceptible to the senses. And therefore it is not that we condemn those philosophers for incompetence or inertia of mind, because they had ascribed the origin of things to rash and fortuitous chance, when rather they showed them eternal and immutable. Hence all things are produced by necessity, and nothing without a cause.[85]

And on this fate Epicurus laid the foundations of his doctrine, although many and more recent writers of the history of philosophy try strenuously to distort and evade. He has brought forward, and ought to do so, many things of which Leucippus and Democritus

[83] Aristot. de gen. et corrupt. I.2.T.I. p. 385. "Democritus and Leucippus, having made forms, make change and origin in them, separation and combination, production and destruction; order and position and change.

[84] Galen. de Element. I. p. 46. "For it underlies all these things, what is the first element, having neither intrinsic whiteness nor blackness nor any other color; neither sweetness, nor bitterness, nor warmth, nor coolness, nor any other quality.

[85] Stob. Ecl. phys. I 8 1.24. Diog. Laert. IX, 35. Cic. quaest. acad. 37. Aristot Phys. VIII. 2.T.I.P. 322. Galen. l c in not. 1, where according to Democritus he relates that qualities have arisen by law. Sext. Empir. Pyrrh. Hypotyp. I.213. adv. Math. VII. 135 sqq. VIII. 184. Led by these arguments, Epicurus would have denied divine reason, relates Lucretius in Book V, and in many passages of song, as also Cicero in his books De Natura Deorum. But here for many reasons the place and scope prevent us from writing vindications of the fate of Epicurus.

have not yet thought; in order that he might either vindicate their doctrine against those things which Socrates, Plato and Aristotle had opposed to it, or might refute and disprove the opinions which they had enunciated about the divine mind.

As an example, I might relate what at the same time illustrates the doctrine of Asclepiades, tries to demonstrate the divine mind of Socrates from wisdom and exceptional structure of parts of the human body, and shows that they have been so prepared that they render the designated utilities and functions[86] to the man. Which Epicurus seems to have undertaken against the opinion of Socrates, when he contended that parts of the body have arisen by fate and eternal law, and that by the same law we are led to use these in this and no other way, but have not designated the divine mind as a use of them.[87]

P. 35.   *Concerning Mind and Soul*

Like all the natural world, the soul owes its origin, structure, and powers to the congregation of atoms. But when philosophers enquired more diligently into the nature of the atoms which constitute soul they thought this could best be elicited from its powers. For according to their opinion, its special power is that whereby it excites motion and life in the animate body.

In the nature of things no matter is conceived which is equipped with greater and more easily mobile power than fire, which on this account they thought to be composed of extremely small and round atoms.[88] The soul, then, like fire, is composed of round, infinitesimally

[86] vid. Xenoph. Memorab. Socrat. lib. I. c. 6.

[87] Lucret. IV. V. 821. sqq Galen. de us. part. I. p. 367. T.I.

[88] Aristot. de anim. I.2.T.I. p. 476. and similarly also Leucippus. "And of these the spheroidal are fire and spirit, and are always able to exchange such rhythms, and to move other things, being moved also themselves, assuming spirit to be that which furnishes motion to animals." Aristotle mentions the same thing about Democritus. Nemes. de nat. hom. c. 2. p. 38 ed. Oxon. We cannot pass over what Epicurus brought forward about this matter more and other than Leucippus and Democritus. Doubtless according to his opinion mind and soul, since the former is the principal part, and at its signal the soul or spirit, in which the moving power is located, would move Mind and spirit owe their origin to the most minute and round atoms, or rather to four different parts, warmth, wind, air, and a certain nameless thing which is composed of the smallest and most mobile atoms, and is the principle and origin of sensation. Vid. Lucret. III. V. 178 sqq. Plutarch: de placit. philosoph. IV. 3. Stob. I,i. Spirit produces motion in us, air rest, heat produces the phenomenon warmth of the body, and the nameless produces sensation. Diog. Laert. x. 63, 66.

small and delicate atoms and does not have its abode fixed in any certain place of the body, but wanders and is distributed through the entire body.[89]

But when we proceed further in scrutinizing the doctrine about the soul, we find that philosophers have thought that those atoms by which the soul becomes formed and animated are transferred into the body through the lungs: and no wonder, when they note what and how great a connection there is between life, and all motions of the body, and respiration, so much so that when the latter is stopped, the former cannot be without danger of destruction. The object of respiration, then, is the production of life. Doubtless external air is filled with those round atoms which in inhalation enter the lungs at the same time as the air, there they are separated, inflate the lungs, and thence prevent them from being compressed and the remaining vital material from being able to be expelled. But if that material can no further resist the surrounding air, the lungs are compressed by it, life departs, and the body dies.[90]

Since in the nature of things, all things which are differentiated exhibit qualities due to their assembly of atoms, and the same is also valid about spirit, we have no reason to wonder since it itself is combined from atoms. Hence Leucippus and Democritus think that reason, and various other faculties, in which spirit excels, can be explained solely by a mixture of round atoms; and that spirit, reason, and fire rejoice in the same component parts.[91] Epicurus modified their opinion, in that he placed a distinction between mind and soul which moves at impulse from the former.[92]

[89] Epicurus conceives the seat of the mind in the breast, but the soul is distributed through the whole body. Lucret. III, V. 138 sqq Diog. Laert. X.66. Hence Plutarch de placit. philos. IV. 4. falsely says the same thing about Democritus, which is refuted from Lucret. III. V. 371 sqq.

[90] Aristot. de respirat. T.I. p 555 c 4 says that spirit and warmth are the same thing, the first forms of the spheroids; and when they are separated from their surrounding and containing medium, he says they help respiration occur For that in the air there is a great number of these, which he now calls also spirit And being inhaled and entering the air, and arousing pressure there, it prevents the spirit from escaping from animals And on this account inhalation and exhalation are life and death For when first the surrounding atmosphere squeezes, not being able to exhale, then death befalls the animals. For death is the destruction of these forms by the pressure of the atmosphere.

Cf Aristot. de anim I, 2.T.I p 478.

[91] Aristot. de anim. I.2, p 479 "For spirit is the same thing as mind.—Mind and fire are the same " Cf. P. 36. not k.

[92] Lucret. III. V. 138 sqq.

P. 36.   *Perception of Objects and Criteria of Truth*

It is sufficiently possible to gather that all perception of objects and truth occurs through the senses, and that this has been perceived and thought by philosophers from the data which have thus far been given. To speak first of Epicurus, he has shown that the senses transcend all fallacy, and that true perception occurs thence. For reason can declare nothing true or false contrary to sensation, for reason itself arises altogether from sensations. Hence reason cannot refute sensation, since it ought only to deny or affirm what already has been adopted by the senses as true or false. But confidence must be had in the senses, because all sensations are spontaneous experiences of reason and faculty, which either adds to things perceived or subtracts what it can. Hence it results that, to each one, that is true which to each one seems so.[93]

But concepts, which can be perceived only by reason and do not occur in the nature of things, are understood wholly by reason, which nevertheless may derive them from concepts of perceptible objects, by analogy, induction, logic, and other faculties of this sort.[94]

Another criterion of truth is that anticipation or prolepsis which occurs from frequent and repeated perception of a certain concept.[95]

[93] Diog Laert. X 32 sq. First he says that perceptions are of truth For he says every perception is irrational and indicative of no recollection For whatever moves by itself, and whatever is moved by something else, can be added or detracted so as to be true or to deceive. —And reason cannot refute sensation, for all reason has been removed from sensation K T.L. Sext Empiric adv logic. II f8 460 Lucret. IV. V 480 sqq where other arguments, wherewith Epicurus sought to bolster up his doctrine, are read outlined in copious words.

[94] Diog Laert I 1 Whence it is necessary to indicate about obscure things from their phenomena For all perceptions also derive from sensations in accordance with circumstance, and analogy, and similarity, and syntheses, contributing something also to reason

[95] Diog. Laert X 33 "They say that prolepsis resembles catalepsis, or correct opinion, or understanding, or general universal knowledge, in which remembrance often appears from without" Sext. Emp. adv. grammat f 57 p. 228. Vid Kindervater's Anmerk. u. Abhand 1. "uber Cicero's Buch " v d Nat d Gott c. 16, 17 T I p 219 Cicero l c brings forward a different concept of prolepsis "what Epicurus calls prolepsis, that is, a certain anticipated information of a thing in the mind, without which nothing can be understood nor questioned, not disputed." It is not likely that Cicero would have said this falsely. Perhaps since the qualities of all things arise from the union of atoms, and the faculties of the soul itself originate from the combination of atoms which constitute it, perhaps, I say, Epicurus assumed that these precognitions also owe their origin to the combination of those round and delicate atoms and does not depend solely on frequent perception of every concept. Some of Cicero's words suggest the same thing, who in the same place calls precognitions inherent or rather innate perceptions impressed on the minds of all by nature herself. This is suggested also by the principles of the whole doctrine, or signification of the word itself.

Experiences, according to the opinion of Epicurus, a third criterion of truth, are not pertinent here.[96]

Now it remains that we should speak briefly about the doctrine of Democritus, which at first glance seems different from that of Epicurus, which we have chiefly described. For Democritus represented cognition, which is performed by the senses, as fluctuating and uncertain, because nothing would really happen to us subject to the senses, since all things which the atoms gather and collect have a nature devoid of all sensible quality.[97] Except those two elements, atoms and empty space, there is really nothing: (P. 31) but qualities, which are subject to the senses, really do not exist, but only by law are perceived as such by the senses.[98] Faith therefore, is to be withheld from them, since they indicate what really is not, and only those things are true which fall under reason.[99]

These things having been explained, this seems to have been proved by us, that Democritus was discussing only about the truth of that which is and which is not, and according to the principles, which he had proposed, he ought to maintain that, except for atoms and empty space, nothing is true. Concerning what they call truth of judgment, we do not know what he thought, but it is likely that his doctrine does not differ from that of Epicurus which we previously related. And I am moved to believe this, because he had promised to add certain sensations in a separate book.[100]

P. 37.   *Concerning the Structure of the Human Body*

Lucretius,[101] as he explains, discusses as follows from the mutual structure of things and of the human body why anything is sweet to some and sour to others.

> "All animals that eat food are compelled
> To differ in their outward form and kind
> By the limit of their members, as in seeds

---

[96] Sext. Emp. adv. logic. I. f. 203. i. p. 412. Diog. Laert. l.c.

[97] Sext. Emp. adv. logic. II. f. 7. p. 459.

[98] Sext. Emp. Pyrrh. Hypotyp. I. 213. adv. mathemat. VII. 135 sqq. advers. mathem. VIII, 184. cf. supra. P. 34. not. q.

[99] Sext. Emp. Pyrrh. hypotyp. I. 213 sqq. advers. mathem. VII, 138.

[100] Sext. Emp. advers. mathem. VII. 136.

[101] Lucret. VI. V. 1031 sqq.

They stand apart and vary in their shape.
'T'is needful intervals should differ, paths,
Openings, and passages which we observe
In all the members, in the palate, mouth.
Some must be smaller therefore, larger some,
Some must be angular and others square.
Many are round, multangular are some.
For as they correspond in kind and motion
Their shapes of openings must differ too,
In various ways, as texture doth demand.
'T'is easy now from these things to know all,
Where fever springs when bile is in excess,
Or otherwise diseases are aroused.
Then the whole body is disturbed and all
Positions of the elements are changed."

P. 38.   *Seed*

Seed is secreted humor, which from the whole body passes into places whence it is excreted at intercourse. Seed therefore is found not only in men but in women also.[102]

P. 39.   *Concerning Sleep*

At the end of this chapter, be it permitted to add those justly celebrated sweet verses in which Lucretius speaks of sleep according to the opinion of Epicurus. What is said about it, coming from Asclepiades, is obscure, and excellently illustrated by these verses.[103]

[102] Lucret. VI. v. 1031 sqq. "For always birth is from both kinds of seed."
[103] Lucret IV. V. 916 sqq.

"Sleep comes first when the power of the soul
Is diffused through the limbs, partly expelled,
And partly crushed, sinks more into the depth.
For then at last the limbs are all dissolved
And flow together; for there is no doubt
'T'is the soul's business evermore to make
Sensation in us, which when sleep prevents,
Then we must think our soul is most disturbed,
And cast abroad; not all; for when should lie
The body drenched in the eternal chill
Of death, and when no silent part of soul

> Rests latent in the limbs, whence, suddenly
> It should burst forth like fire from much ashes "

But how the soul can be disturbed and the body languish he undertakes to explain in these words·

> "First from without the body must be touched
> Nearby with airy breezes, soothed, and lulled,
> With frequent beat Likewise the inner part
> The same air strikes in breathing, when the breath,
> Drawn and exhaled, in the same way is beaten.
> And the blows come through tiny openings
> To the first parts and the first elements,
> Like ruin gradually through our limbs.
> For the positions of the elements
> Of body and of mind are all disturbed,
> So that a portion of the soul is thence
> Expelled and hidden deeply sinks within.
> Part also, scattered through the limbs, cannot
> Be reunited or in motion share.
> For nature glides between the paths and ways.
> Therefore sensation goes a changing course;
> And since 't'is not as if what props the limbs
> Were the weak body; all the members fail.
> Arms, eyelids drop, and the weak hams relax "

> "Sleep follows food, because what the air does,
> Food does the same, passing through all the veins.
> And a much deeper sleep arises thence
> Than even the weary knows; because when most
> The body shows itself disturbed with toil
> For the same reason is the soul downcast
> Deeper and farther outcast in the world
> And more divided and distract within "

Chapter VI

THE PHILOSOPHIC AND PHYSIOLOGIC DOCTRINE
OF ASCLEPIADES

P. 40.   *Introduction*

Whoever is disposed to interpret the doctrine of Asclepiades, which he established about philosophy and physiology, ought first to illustrate what are pores, tumors, incompact elements, and subtile spirit. [104] If he does not do this, he cannot fail to fall into devious and inextricable mazes, whence there is neither salvation nor refuge. Doubtless he built the whole system which he established on these principles. It seems therefore to be in order first to engage in explaining his principles, which are obscurely narrated by the ancients, in order that we may then be able more distinctly and correctly to pass judgment on what he taught in medicine.

Asclepiades ought to be numbered among those philosophers who consider atoms the elements of things, and although his doctrine has been handed down to us defective by the ancients, it can best and ought to be illustrated by their theories, which to this end we narrated in the fifth chapter.

P. 41.   *Elements of Philosophy*

The theory proposed by Asclepiades concerning the elements of things is read described in these words in Caelius Aurelianus:[105]

"The elements of all bodies which we perceive in the whole world are the corpuscles,[106] which, in that state in which they do not yet constitute sensible objects, enjoy no quality nor sensation but can be perceived only by the reason. They move perpetually, and by their

---

[104] Galen. in libr III. Hippoc de morb vulgar. Comm I T. V. p 396.

[105] Cael. Aurel I morb. acut C. 14 p. 41

[106] Fabricius ad Sext Empir Pyrrhon Hypotyp III 4 f 32. p 136 notes that C Amasanius the Epicurean, whom Cicero (Acad quaest I 2 Tuscul quaest. IV 3) testifies was the first to have written in Latin about philosophy, used corpuscles instead of the Greek atoms. Caelius Aurelianus I 1 speaks promiscuously about the atoms or corpuscles of Asclepiades. Celsus also in introd proposes corpuscles. In Galen elements and masses mean elements, as also in Sext Empiric I 1 and adv Phys I f 563 p 621 Fabric ad Sext Emp. Pyrrh. Hypotyp. I c cites a passage from Clem (recognit. VIII 15) where "masses" of Asclepiades are translated by "tumors" or "elations." Cf Gassendi animad. in Epicur. Phil. T.I. p. 177 sqq.).

concourse and mutual impact are broken into minute particles of various form and size, which, when they come together, in accordance with their various form and size, compose diverse bodies, now subject to the senses and endowed with qualities."[107]

It is clear that the elements of Asclepiades do not correspond with those which we have previously described of Democritus and of Epicurus, for their elements are most minute and cannot be divided into any smaller particles (P. 31). But, according to the opinion of Asclepiades, they are broken and undergo multiple dissolution. Which difference doubtless has wholly arisen from the carelessness of scribes, who neglected the distinction which Asclepiades, equally with Epicurus (P. 31. not. 79.), made between atoms, compounds, and bodies.[108]

The compounds, which themselves have arisen from combination of atoms, can be seen to be wholly divisible. Relying on this distinc-

---

[107] Caelius Aurel: "For as elements of a body he had first established corpuscles understood in the sense of atoms" (Sext. Empir. adv. Log II. f. 210 p 499. "perceptible masses.") adv. Geometr. f. 5. p. 211 in Log Theoret. "without any habitual quality" or experience of contact, (Galen. de differ. morb. T. III. p. 199, as in many other places) and from the beginning accompanied, eternally in motion, which, broken by their impingements, by mutual blows are divided into infinite fragments of parts, differing in size and form: (Sext. Emp. Pyrrh. Hypotyp. III. 4. f 33. p. 136: broken elements Galen. Introd. p. 375. T. IV) which by returning attached or joined to each other, make all perceptible objects, having in themselves the power of change, either in their size, or number, or form, or arrangement)*

*A suggestion of "splitting the molecules and rearranging them."

[108] Galen. de Theriac ad Pison T. II. p 462 sq. "For if, according to Epicurus and Democritus, all things are made from atoms and empty space, or from certain masses and pores according to the physician Asclepiades; thus they are changing the names only, and say masses instead of atoms and pores instead of empty space," Ackerman (instit. hist medic. CXV. P. 189 p. 135), against this passage of Galen, thinks that the syncrises or compounds of Epicurus were rather called masses by Asclepiades. And this is a shrewd suspicion. For it is very likely that scribes neglected the distinction which Asclepiades established between atoms, compounds, and bodies. Whence it has resulted that they attributed both the names and the qualities promiscuously either to corpuscles or to concretions. Doubtless Galen is also to be accused of the same negligence. For corpuscles mean rather elements. De element. lib. II. p. 58. T. I· clearly from this are distinguished masses and pores and elements. But what pertains to the word mass, Eusebius clearly teaches, praep. evangel XIV, that this was first employed by Heracleides Ponticus, whom Asclepiades followed in this respect. And of these they say the indivisible one the followers of Diodorus named; but they say that Heracleides gave them another name, calling them masses, by which name Asclepiades the physician also received them From this passage we can explain admirably whence it has happened that in many places Sextus Empiricus and Galen at the same time mention Heracleides Ponticus and Asclepiades, so far as each differs from Epicurus and Democritus Vid. Sext. Empir. Pyrrhon Hypotyp. III. 4. p 136. adv. Phys. I. f. 363. p. 621. adv. Phys. II. f. 318. p. 686. Galen. de memor. spasm. et rigor. T. III. p. 369.

tion we shall engage in differentiating qualities, which we assign to atoms and compounds, and so we shall best look out that we are not deceived by the errors of the scribes.

There are, then, those corpuscles, elements of things, infinitely small, which can be conceived by reason only: they are indivisible:[109] they possess all qualities:[110] they are packed with an infinite number of forms. They are perpetually in motion, they come together, and first form concretions: which in turn collide and then form new concretions or perceptible objects, now equipped with faculties and qualities, so that they are perceived by our senses. (P. 31)

P. 42.   *How the Qualities of Perceptible Objects Arise*

Caelius describes the way in which Asclepiades undertook to explain the way in which corpuscles, combining into perceptible objects, are endowed with qualities, speaking as follows:

Says he, "There would seem to lack no reason why they should make bodies of no quality. For the parts follow one pattern, the whole follows another: in short silver is white, but its filings black; goat's horn is black, but its powder is white."

By these examples Asclepiades wished to demonstrate nothing else

[109] In Galen and Sextus Empiricus there often occur "incomplete elements, incomplete atoms." Galen de differ. morbor. T III. p. 199. Sext Emp pyrrh. Hypotyp. l. c I remain doubtful about the meaning of this term. Very likely "incomplete elements" means the same as "imperfect elements", and as translators of Galen and Sextus by "incompact" or "incomposed". moreover these elements agree admirably with those "indivisible elements" of Democritus and Epicurus (P. 31). But the same elements in Caelius Aurelianus, Galen, and Sextus Empiricus would be considered as divisible and fragile (P. 41. not 111.): no doubt the same carelessness is seen to exist here for which we have already condemned scribes who did not sufficiently understand the distinction, established by Epicurus and Asclepiades, between corpuscles and concretions: whence it has resulted that they wrongly applied to concretions the term "incomplete", which in corpuscles would indicate only indivisible.—But perhaps "incomplete" is more rightly explained as "various", so that "incomplete masses" are "masses differing in size and form." So we understand "incomplete masses" in Sext. Emp. adv. Phys. II. f. 318. p 686. Finally perhaps "incomplete elements" are elements not joined together, which flit around singly everywhere in empty space eternally in motion. Perhaps now Le Clerc (Hist de Méd II. 3. 5.) meant to designate this meaning of the words, rendering thus "detached elements," or "those which do not agree together."

[110] Opposed is Sextus Empiricus, who (Pyrrhon. Hypotyp. III. 4 p. 136) names the "active element" of Asclepiades (adv. Phys II f 3, 8 p 686) as the "experienced element", in which he had followed Heracleides Ponticus but faith is not to be lost in Caelius and Galen, who describe those elements as containing no qualities, which they rather ascribe, and that rightly, to concretions or perceptible objects (P. 41. not 111.) Beyond doubt also Sextus exchanged atoms and compounds, and assigned to the former qualities which ought to be ascribed only to the latter.

except that the qualities of objects, as they meet our senses, derive only from an assemblage of molecules which were different, for just as corpuscles differ from one another, so their assemblages are different. (P. 32)

On these principles, concerning which we have spoken as fully as possible, Asclepiades built the doctrine which he established about the elements and the structure of living bodies and about the principle of them which we call rational; about health, disease, and things which, demonstrated therefrom, pertain to medical science: in short everything about which it is now our purpose to discuss individually.

P. 43.   *Elements of Living Bodies*

The elements of living bodies are the same corpuscles which constitute all perceptible objects. From their combination and attachment passages arise, which, according to the size, form, position, and arrangement of the corpuscles, are themselves wider or narrower, or shaped in one way or another. The narrowest, like the corpuscles themselves, are comprehended only by the reason, but cannot be perceived by the senses. Corpuscles pass between the walls of the meatuses, between the wider larger, between the narrower smaller, and between the narrowest smallest (P. 37.[111]).

P. 44.   *Health, Disease, Cure*

Since these things are so, it is not hard to be perceived what concept Asclepiades imagined of health and disease. Health is when the corpuscles pass through the passages in an equal manner and intercepted by no impediments: disease is when that relation, which in a healthy state subsists between the passages and the moving corpuscles, is impaired and impediments are present which disturb their equal motion: cure is when that relation, which is requisite for

[111] Cael. Aurel l c p. 42 "passages are also made from the combination of corpuscles, perceptible by the reason, differing in size and form." Galen Introd. T IV p. 375 "according to Asclepiades the human elements are fragmented corpuscles and passages " De Theriac. ad Pison. To II p 458. Sext Emp adv Geometr f. 5. p 311 "some passages are perceptible in us, differing from one another in size—everywhere moist parts and air are found in place of theoretical molecules." In the same Sextus adv Logic II f. 220 p 499 there occur "perceptible porosities", which term Celsus doubtless intended to designate from the outset when he made mention of "invisible foramina", which, like porosities of the Greeks, it appears from these passages, is not spoken promiscuously but only of the narrowest openings. Cael. Aurel. l c calls those smallest corpuscles passing through foramina spirit (tenuous, air Sext. Emp. l c.) others of a more solid nature, juices or liquids (fluid. Sext. Emp I.1.)

the healthy state, is restored by treatment so that the motion of the corpuscles can proceed according to the laws of health.[112]

Well! these are the "futile and remarkable"[113] atoms of Asclepiades; that is the "elementary Asclepiadean doctrine", which Galen, and many blinded by his authority and prestige, so ambitiously rebuke. But if we duly examine this whole matter, swearing to the words of no biassed person and influenced by no prejudiced opinions, we cannot fail to confess that that doctrine is not so futile that it is not daily recognized by us. What then?

Are the corpuscles constituting parts of the animal body what we call solids? Are meatuses vessels? Are flowing corpuscles fluids or humors? He seems to have declared those foramina invisible not merely because he was influenced by too great a desire of stabilizing his system. For he understands that either the vessels are very small or the interstices which intervene between the fibres and the cellular tissue. But particularly Asclepiades endured Galen's rebukes and detractions because, led by those principles, he gathered his strength, acting both in the whole realm of nature and in the living body: wherefore if rightly he ought to be contemned, let us now despise him.

P. 45.   *Concept of Asclepiades Concerning*
                Nature and her Powers

Although Asclepiades, equally with Democritus and Epicurus, decided that there is nothing except corpuscles and empty space which can be either an element or some divine power, cultivator or catalyst of nature: yet it can easily be perceived that the origin of things ought to be explained from eternal law, in which the elements are contained. Therefore he thinks that nothing arises by rash fate, but that everything must necessarily be created, and nothing without a cause.[114] The elements rejoice in necessity and eternal law: by

[112] Galen nat. med lib. IV. p 77. T. IV. "Asclepiades assumes that our health consists in a certain symmetry of the pores, and disease in asymmetry, and undertakes the therapeutic approach to the former symmetry of the pores " De Hippocr. et Platon decret. lib V. p. 288. T I Cael. Aurel. l c. "through which duct is the passage of the juice running in its customary meatus; if it were checked by no obstacle, health would continue, but if obstructed by stasis of the corpuscles, it makes diseases "

[113] Galen de natural. facult. I. p 91 sqq. To I de Element. lib. II p 58. To. I.

[114] Cael Aurel. l c p 43: "Wrongly, therefore, and contrary to the principles of philosophy", Le Clerc (Hist de méd. II 3, 5) accuses that this principle was taken by Caelius from the philosophy of the Stoics and falsely introduced into the opinions of Asclepiades

necessity they move, and combine, and constitute all things that are perceived by us. Hence we can understand him who could say that "nature is nothing else than body or its motion."[115]

Doubtless, according to the principles of his doctrine he denies rational and divine nature, administering everything in the natural world. But in the corpuscles and their motion is located the cause from which all things, which are, originate. (P. 34)

For the same reason also he denies nature thriving in the living body and administering its functions. For from the things which we have described (P. 41) we know that Asclepiades had concluded that the elementary corpuscles enjoy no qualities which would arise only in those which we have shown in the nature of things from the combination of corpuscles. Therefore the parts of the living body are subject to the same necessity, whereby all things were placed in the world: we are bound by the same law that we should use these in this and no other way. The powers which we note in the body derive from the same law. There are no intrinsic and innate powers.[116] P. 34.

P. 46.   *Digestion   of   Foods*

In order that we may rightly judge concerning this function of the animal body according to the doctrine of Asclepiades, we ought to know that his material was immutable and unalterable, and that it could undergo no other change except what takes place in a varied and changed connection, position, and arrangement of molecules. The molecules themselves cannot be changed: for they are indivisible, unaffectable, and endowed with no qualities. P. 33.[117]

It is clear, therefore, that Asclepiades, in order that he might explain digestion, could not take refuge in putrefaction, which according to statements of physicians requires, as I may say, internal change of particular constituents: nor, like Hippocrates, in warmth, which he would deny to be innate in us. (P. 45). Rather he thinks that the foods are digested and dissolved in the stomach, and not

[115] Cael Aurel. l.c.

[116] Galen. de us. part. XI. p. 489. T. I where, from the wise and excellent structure of the teeth, he endeavors to prove divine purpose against Asclepiades, whereby they were formed and were designated for the use of men. Cf. Natural. Facult. I. p. 91 sqq. T. I. De Tremor. palp et rigor. T. 3. P. 369. For Asclepiades placed warmth alone, but no power as innate or intrinsic.

[117] De. differ morbor. T. III. p. 199. "For it is possible for the atom itself, to have some experience, but only in synthesis and in endurance."

cooked, but the crude material, as it is assumed to be, is carried into the entire body.[118] Doubtless the foods we ingest undergo no other change in the stomach except solution into those elementary corpuscles of no quality, and these, on account of their different shape and size are conducted and directed in different ways, and so constitute different parts of the body.[119]

From a certain passage of Galen it seems to me more than sufficiently clear that, besides Asclepiades, he wished to prove his own opinion by experience, when he said that foods, if we either take account of eructations arising from them as they delay in the stomach, or if we note what are ejected by vomiting or come into sight after dissection of the stomach, do not show the slightest signs of digestion or of internal change, so that rather of them, even though they are still in the stomach, the same savor can be perceived as that which is perceived as soon as they are consumed.[120]

[118] Cels. in introduct. Galen. definit. medic. T. IV. p. 393.

[119] Cael. Aurel. l c. p. 44: "and that there is no other digestion in us, but that crude solution of foods is produced in the abdomen and goes through individual parts of the body, so that it is seen to penetrate through all thin places, what is called tenuous substance, but which we understand as spirit.—And he does not say it is of a warm quality, nor of a cold, nor that it has any other sense of touch, but by way of the receptacles of nutrition, now made an artery, now a nerve, now a vein, now flesh. The place for these is involved in many obscurities, and very likely it labors with a certain defect, which doubtless seems to lie concealed in those words· "so that it seems to penetrate through all thin places." Perhaps we can administer some remedy if instead of "seen" we read "life." For according to Asclepiades, as we shall show a little further below, just as according to Democritus and Epicurus (P. 35), on that tenuous substance depend life, warmth, respiration, and spirit. The sense, then, of that passage of Caelius is this: "in the stomach foods are dissolved into corpuscles, of which individuals go to individual parts of the body, and there form nerves, arteries, and all parts of the body. But the most tenuous go to all parts of the body as life, vital substance, and spirit, because there are life and warmth in all. And the words which follow,—"and do not make flesh",—are understood not of the spirit, but of the nutrient corpuscles. It was already suspected that an error underlies these Caelian words, by Ammannus, who noted in the margin that perhaps "tenuous ways ought to be read instead of tenuous life." But that most tenuous material not only travels through tenuous and subtile ways, but imparts life and warmth to all parts of the body. Finally, those words "individual parts of the body" and "all tenuous passages" do not rightly correspond. For the sense is· "as through individual passages the nutrient bodies pass, so, through them all, the spirit passes."

[120] Galen. de natur. facult. III. p. 111 T. I. "And Asclepiades is absurd when he says that the quality of the digested foods appears sometimes in the eructations, sometimes in the vomitus, sometimes in dissections. For this introduces the phenomena of the body and of the intestine into digestion. This is as naive as when we hear the ancients say that foods are changed to the useful in the stomach, it seems to be not inquiring about function but about useful taste. Cf. with this passage another which exists in fragm. Galen. Comment. II. in lib. Hippocr. de alimento., where the same opinion is read expressed in almost the same words.

Here we cannot pass over what Asclepiades warned against Erasistratus concerning digestion and distribution of food through the entire body. Doubtless according to Erasistratus foods digested in the stomach are carried through the veins to all parts of the body. Erasistratus thinks that then the veins, when the nutrient fluid is evacuated, become either empty or, if they immediately receive a new afflux of it, become full. But Asclepiades warns that the veins can be not only empty or full, but also collapsed.[121]

P. 47.   *Concerning Respiration*

The lungs according to Asclepiades, are compared with a funnel: and if we wish to find the likeness, we must think the funnel inverted, whose terminus runs into the trachea at the apex, but its lumen more nearly equals the lungs.

The cause of respiration, he says, is that (tenuous) spirit composed of the minutest corpuscles, which is much more subtile and lighter than external air: whence it results that atmospheric air, being heavier and thicker, can enter the lungs. In this way, then, inhalation is produced. Thus the lungs are filled with external air, so that they can be distended no more: therefore the air goes out, and exhalation is produced. But that most subtile material, which is dissolved and dissipated in the external air, remains in the chest: whence it results that again atmospheric air can enter.

This action of the lungs he compares with that which is noted in cupping-glasses, which, as they are applied, have within them attenuated air; but, if they are withdrawn, they receive into themselves the heavier external air.[122]

[121] Galen. de natur. facult. II p 98. T. I. "And he (Erasistratus) thinks that if anything flows away from the veins one of two things is true, either that the vein is empty or that it is flowing continuously, filling the vacancy. But Asclepiades says that not one of two but one of three things must be said to ensue when the veins have been emptied, either they remain empty, or they are refilled, or the vessel collapses. for this is true of reeds and tubes when they are immersed in water, if their tunics collapse.

[122] Plutarch de placit philos IV. 22 "Asclepiades assumes that the lungs are the cause of respiration in the thorax. Towards them the external air flows and is carried, being thicker, and is again expelled " cf Galen de hist. philos T. IV p 435, where the opinion of Asclepiades is shown outlined in almost the same words; and hence it is very likely, which already several have suspected, that the work of Plutarch and of Galen was written by one and the same author Lionardo di Capua (Raggion. v. p 369) thinks that Asclepiades, explaining respiration in this way, had already perceived the so-called elastic force which is attributed to air. But nothing of this sort is clear, from the writers themselves. (Cf. Bianchini. la med. d'Ascl. disc II. P. X)

The use of respiration is the generation or production of spirit, a thing which we shall demonstrate in several ways in the following paragraph, when our discourse will be about spirit.[123] P. 35.

But Asclepiades thinks that respiration obeys our desire, the narrowest passages of the lungs being contracted subject to the will.[124]

P. 48.   *Concerning Spirit and Mind*

This discipline of Asclepiades was handed down to us by our elders in defective and obscure form, and a clearer light ought to be sought from those doctrines of Democritus and Epicurus which we have explained above. (P. 35.).

We know already that Asclepiades had determined nothing except those elements, corpuscles and empty space: we know that he had denied to us innate powers which, like all qualities of things owe their origin to the combination of corpuscles. From these already it can be understood that spirit and mind have not been able to devise for themselves their own powers, different from matter and not understood by the mind;[125] but that matter was formed from the same elements from corpuscles.

From our outline of the philosophy of Democritus and of Epicurus (P. 35) we have seen that those philosophers have been persuaded that spirit is composed of the most tenuous and round corpuscles. Asclepiades is of the same opinion, and equally with them thinks that life depends on those corpuscles, motion, sensation, and animal heat, and that they are carried into the body by respiration and wander through the entire body.[126]

[123] Galen. de usu respirat. p 153. T. III.

[124] Galen. Hist. phil. l.c. "Voluntary respiration takes place in the passages of the lungs. For our supposition assumes this."

[125] Galen de plenitud. p. 346. T. III

[126] Since most of the doctrine of Asclepiades is based on the concept of spirit, which he formed, nothing ought to be more precious to us than now to inquire into it more diligently. That spirit which Asclepiades called tenuous substance (Cael. Aurel morb. chron. III. 4. p. 455) which is combined of the most tenuous corpuscles (Cael Aurel morb. acut. I 15. p. 48 and p. 57) is carried into the body by respiration (P. 47), but not by respiration alone, but also by foods dissolved and digested in the stomach into elementary corpuscles (P. 46, not. y). Anything ingested into the body tends to the heart, because it, together with the blood, ministers to all parts of the body. (Cael Aurel morb. acut II. 34 p. 164) Then it subserves all the functions which pertain to spirit and life. Upon it depends the warmth in the animal body Hence Caelius calls mind itself fervor (morb acut I. 15 p. 46 and 48.). Sensation is dependent on it, and it is part of the reason why we can feel external things. Hence we can explain why pains are ascribed to it. (Cael Aurel. morb. acut. I. 15. p 57.) and all affections

P. 49.   *Concerning the Knowledge of Things*
                      and Criteria of Truth

In this Asclepiades seems to have followed Democritus, when he
proved knowledge through the senses as transient and uncertain
(P. 36). For although, equally with him, he determined nothing beyond those two elements, which actually would be everything, when
it was considered, which is observed in perceptible objects, only to
originate from combination of corpuscles, which themselves were
being changed with every changed moment of time. He could not
fail to be persuaded that the senses tell us nothing of truth.[127]
He seems to have wished to prove this from colors; for if these are
mixed gradually, he would not be able to discern the shades which
gradually are formed as changes.[128] But whether Asclepiades understood by tenuous material to be named a quarter of those minutest
corpuscles in which, according to Epicurus, is located the element of
sensation (P. 35.not.88), is not sufficiently clear, since his scribes say
nothing about this. At the end of this disquisition, I am glad to give

---

which afflict it, so that more often it will be a place to turn to in the whole body. Moreover
there derives from it the harmony which operates between the various parts of the body
(Cael. Aurel morb. chr. IV. 4. p. 455.) From this disquisition it is understood why the sectarians of Asclepiades (Galen. natur. facult. I. p. 90, 91.) when of nature they sought some
characteristic or function, always turned to it. It is now clear why Asclepiades denied that
there is a kingdom of the mind established anywhere in the body. (Cael. Aurel. ac morb. I.
14. p. 45) It is clearer from a certain passage of Tertullian (de anima c. 15), from which we
can learn that perhaps Asclepiades wished us to know by heart his opinion about the wandering abode of the soul against his coeval philosophers, especially against the Stoics, whose
common opinion it was; (Lips. physiol Stoic III. 18. Gataker. ad M. Anton W 3) and prove
it by experiments and experience. These are the words of Tertullian "Both Protagoras and
Apollodorus and Chrysippus know these things, so that Asclepiades, restrained by them, seeks
his own goats bleating without a heart and drives away his flies flitting without a head. Asclepiades seems to have been deserted by his sectarians, who maintained that the soul is
diffused through the entire body, but so that it is attached more to one than to another
member" (Galen de Hist. phil p. 426. T. IV. XIX 254.) That most tenuous material has
its location in the narrowest meatuses of the body. (Cael. Aurel. I. morb. acut. 15. p. 57).
But whether by tenuous material Asclepiades understood that nameless fourth part of the
smallest corpuscles in which, according to Epicurus (P. 35 not. 88), the principle of sensation
is located, is not sufficiently clear, since the scribes report nothing about this.

[127] Sext. Emp adv. Logic II. f. 7. p. 459. Plato, saying that no truth can be judged by
the senses, since there are always appearances but never being (reality), like a river flowing
from Asia. These things occur twice, but do not persist; as also Asclepiades said, showing
two on account of the clearness of the stream.

[128] Sext. Emp. adv. Log. I f. 91. p. 338.

this comment, that Asclepiades attributed to spirit all the functions which more recent authors ascribe to nerves.

Nevertheless sensations are the only ways whereby we can perceive external objects and what fall among these, since reason of itself does nothing, and is dependent on action of the senses.[129] He did not wish to eliminate all sensation from reason, but only to deny that which was different from the action and substance of the senses.[130] But we acquire concepts of concealed objects by repeated function of the senses, analogy, induction, memory, and other function of the senses of this sort.[131]

If we survey at a glance what has been reported thus far, we find this demonstrated, that Asclepiades denied peculiar powers and virtues of the mind, different from the senses. The mind emerges from the exercise of the senses, which, although worthy of no confidence, nevertheless furnish us certain concepts through more frequent and repeated activity. From these concepts the mind prepares for itself concepts of concealed objects by inferences from similars to similars.

On the heel of this discussion, let us immediately give warning of what too often is wont to happen, that pupils, either led by ignorance or inflamed by sectarian ambition, distort and twist their teachers' dogmata in many ways, and that this happened to Asclepiades also. Galen relates that there were some of his sectarians who removed all virtue of the mind, whereby it judges, nay did not shame to confess that we are led, like sheep, by the affects of the senses and cannot

---

[129] Sext. Emp. adv. Log. I. f. 201. 2 p. 412. Former criteria seem not to have been far from perception of the truth. Antiochus from the Academy first made this observation, but someone else wrote it later. He was persuaded that perceptions are really and truly anticipatory. But we do not wholly comprehend anything by reason For Antiochus from these things is likely to have made the first statement, and then that Asclepiades the physician repeated it. Cf. id. adv. Log. I. f. 380 p. 445.

[130] Cael. Aurel. I. acut. morb. 24. p. 45. "for he says that spirit is nothing else than an assemblage of all the sensations." Galen. defin. med. p. 393. T. IV.

[131] Cael Aurel. l. c "the understanding of concealed or latent objects is accomplished by relaxing movement of the senses, which is due to occurring sensations and to antecedent perception." Galen (natur. facult. I. p. 91. T. I) speaks more distinctly: "In respect to the others (sectarians of Asclepiades), neither is there anything of these in their natures, nor any innate perception in their spirit from the beginning, either of agreement, or of conflict, or of separation, or of union, or of just, or of unjust, or of beautiful, or of ugly; but from perception and through perception they say everything happens to us, and dwells living in some imaginations and memories." Hence it is clear what it is that Caelius mentions l c: "that memory is produced through alternating exercise of the senses."

deny or repudiate anything. To the same authors fortitude, prudence, temperance, moderation are mere trifles: and we do not love ourselves or our children: we care nothing for the gods: and the same authors despise auguries, dreams, portents, and all astrology.[132]

P. 50.   *Concerning Secretion*

Asclepiades denies secretion, which, according to the opinion of most physicians, is accomplished by the powers of nature in the healthy animal's body and he can supersede them on account of the doctrine which he established about the living body, and chiefly about the digestion of foods.

As soon as we speak of the reason why urine is secreted into the bladder, Asclepiades thinks that humors, which we ingest into the stomach, are there dissolved into breath and vapors, carried through passages into the bladder, there collected, and expelled as fluids which we call urine.[133]

It seems altogether remarkable that Asclepiades deprived the kidneys of all functions: but Le Clerc[134] has already conjectured that perhaps near them he had merely placed that shorter passage to the bladder, doubtless relying on the experience that often, not long after the ingestion of fluids, we find the urinary bladder full. This opinion, which is also favored by many of the moderns, is greatly approved. To this is added that as Asclepiades himself has said, we cannot rightly judge about it, since Galen prefers to talk about his sectarians.

It is probable that Asclepiades had persuaded himself the same about the other secretions. For Galen relates that he believed that bile is produced in the passages themselves, but not secreted nor otherwise modified, from black bile and the spleen.[135] From these things which we have ascertained about the separation of urine, I gather that Asclepiades undoubtedly imagined that in the same way, from foods digested in the stomach, the particles which constitute

---

[132] Galen natural. facult. l. c.

[133] Galen natural. facult 1 c "for he means that the putrefying fluid, dissolving into atoms, is distributed into the bladder; and then from that again, combining together, it thus resumes its original form, and becomes again simply moisture from atoms."

[134] Hist de Medic. II. 3 8

[135] Galen. de natur facult. l.c. p. 92. cf o. P. 52. not. 2.

either yellow or black bile are carried either to the liver or the spleen, there collected, and compose and constitute both biles.[136]

P. 51.   *Other Secretions*

According to the opinion of Asclepiades, semen is the reproductive fluid which is excreted[137] in sex relations and owes its origin to the same corpuscles from which the whole human body is composed. It is produced from foods digested in the same way as all the other so-called secretory fluids, urine, bile, black bile, and mucus.[138]

P. 52.   *Concerning Sleep*

Asclepiades explains sleep from that material which he called most tenuous; doubtless he had been taught by experience that in sleep sensations cease, whose power lies in that material; that in sleep the body is tired and weary, which is from material diminished by labors and other causes. (P. 39. P. 48. not. 126.)[139]

P. 53.   *He Denies the Power of Nature from*
                   the Structure of Tendons

From many things which we have hitherto stated, we have already ascertained that an important part of the doctrine of Asclepiades

[136] It is noted that, for accomplishing the functions of the body, Galen had established certain perpetually flourishing forces, altering, excreting, attracting, and retaining. Asclepiades, relying on the principles of the doctrine to which he had given his name, could enunciate nothing of this sort, and denied them uterus, kidneys, spleen, stomach, liver, and other parts of the body. (Galen. de natur. facult III p 114 T. I). It is a pleasure to mention here that in this Asclepiades departed from Epicurus, who tried to prove these powers fundamental according to his doctrine. In many places Galen endeavors to demonstrate this by an example taken from the magnet and iron Then he adds (de natural. facult. I p 93 T. I) "And he says that in the bodies of animals both absorptions occur, and eliminations of excrements, and the energies of the purgative drugs. But Asclepiades, suspecting both that the so-called cause was untrustworthy and finding no other trace of elements on which he could rely, was not ashamed to say that nothing is wholly attracted by anything "

[137] Galen definit medic T. IV. p. 401. The reproductive fluid excreted in sex relations.

[138] The classic passage on this subject is read in Octav Horatian (lib IV p. 105) (edit. Argent 1532) "But Asclepiades, concurring, says that the essence both of the universal seed of men and of animals is spirit, likewise to be understood as of the principal corpuscle· but the acidity of meat underlies it, that is new food received or new nourishment thereafter. For he wishes returns to be made from crude materials so that the scattered material of received food may be distributed through all parts and regions of the body "

[139] Cael Aurel. I l c p 45. "For sleep always indicates that the spirits have become sensible by thickening " What is to be understood by this thickening is best revealed by those verses of Lucretius which we have taken pains to quote at the end of P. 39.

lies in the fact that he established no powers in the whole nature of things by which things are either effected or formed. Hence he could not also fail to remove also every power of nature whereby parts of the living body were designated to perform certain functions, and formed to this end. (P. 45)

This opinion is confirmed by that which Asclepiades teaches about the structure of tendons. For he denies that they were formed by a wise and foreseeing nature either thicker or thinner in order that they might perform their designated duty, but rather that their slenderness or thickness depend on the varying way in which they are exercised.*[140]

P. 54.   Concerning the Structure of Vessels Going from Heart to Lungs

From Galen's writings[141] it is known that the ancients considered that only veins enter the right sinus of the heart, and only arteries enter the left sinus. They found, however, that that vessel going from the right ventricle to the lungs, which we call the pulmonary artery, is more like the arteries, in that it is itself more slender than other arteries in the whole body. But those vessels extending from the lungs to the left atrium, which to us are pulmonary veins, are more of a venous nature, though they are themselves thicker than other veins which go through the whole body.

Galen, who calls the former arterial veins, but the latter venous arteries, in this structure of the vessels also admires wise nature. But Asclepiades takes refuge in the motion which is in the lungs. Doubtless the arteries move with a double motion, of which one is in themselves and the other in the lungs: hence they are weaker than the other arteries of the body. But whereas the veins of the whole body

---

* His explanation is not teleological, but adaptive.

[140] Galen de us part. I. p. 378 T. I. "Therefore it seems to these men, (sectarians of Asclepiades and Epicurus), that the tendons became thick because their functions were strong, and slender because their functions were weak; but they were compelled to become thu and so by their uses in life, and the size of the tendons corresponds to the quantity of the motion. And of those who exercise, it is likely, they grow longer and thicker; and of those who are idle they atrophy and shrink; for it is better that of the strong functions the tendons are strong and thick, and of the weak functions that they are slender and feeble Thus, he says, they are changed by nature; for monkeys do not have fingers for exercise, but, as was said before, the fingers inevitably follow the exercise, on account of being well nourished."

[141] Galen. de us. part. VI. p. 435 T. I.

are without any motion, those in the lungs move, and thence become thicker. Galen seems to imply this in the very words of Asclepiades.[142]

For he says in the lung only of all the organs the arteries move with a double motion, one which they have from their own nature, evidently pulsating, and one from the respiration shaking the lung, wholly expanded, then the arteries thin out in the other parts, moving sufficiently with their own proper motion, and on this account becoming well-nourished and strong.

And the veins he says in the whole animal remain motionless, like some lazy and unexercised slave, and justly they atrophy. But those in the lung, performing the motion of the viscera, grow thick like those moderately exercised.

P. 55.   *Certain Thoughts About the Foetus*

There was a conflict between the philosophers and the physicians whether the foetus, flourishing in the uterus, is an animal, or not an animal, and rather to be compared with the vegetation of plants.[143] Asclepiades says it is neither animal nor non-animal, but comparable to the dormant: for as the latter possess sensations but do not use them, so is that also which is borne in the uterus.[144]

While the foetus is being formed in the uterus, declares Asclepiades, in males, because they are warmest, the limbs are distinguished on the twenty-sixth day and rendered perfect on the fiftieth, but certain ones are formed even within this space of time: but females begin within two months, and are completed in the fourth month, since they are cooler: but other animals, from easy union of elements, are equally all begun and finished.[145]

Multiple Pregnancies

Concerning twins and triplets Galen reports that Asclepiades ascribed their conception to the nature of the seed; for as barley is

---

[142] Galen. de us part. VI. p. 436. T. I.

[143] Galen hist. phil. p. 436 T. IV.

[144] Galen. defin. med. p. 402. T. IV. Asclepiades says the embryo is neither animal nor non-animal, but like the dormant; for they have senses but do not use them.

[145] Galen Hist. phil. p 437. T. IV. Asclepiades says of males, because their temperament is warmer, their articulation occurs on the twenty-sixth day, and is completed on the fiftieth day; but of females the articulation occurs in two months, on account of their lack of warmth.

found which produces ears of two and three rows, so there is highly
fertile seed which produces two or more embryos.[146]

P. 56.   *He Refutes the Popular Opinion About the Cause of Old Age*

Galen relates that the Stoics and physicians equally all have
agreed in this, that old age comes from lack of warmth, and that
those who have more warmth grow old later. But Asclepiades thinks
contrary to them that the Aethiopians become old faster, even in
their sixtieth year, since their bodies are too much burned by the
heat of the sun; but that Britons on the contrary die in their hun-
dredth year and later; for they inhabit a cold region. The Aethiopians, whom continually the sun relaxes, relax themselves; but the
Britons have a tough body and live the longer life.[147]

P. 57. 1.   *Conclusions*

Sextus Empiricus reports that Asclepiades stated, judging about
the old and the young, that the latter far surpass the former in intelligence and shrewdness of mind, although old men have more experience than young.[148] Doubtless Asclepiades meant by these words
nothing else than that age is no guarantee of truth or falsehood.

2. As for what remains, let us add here the opinion of Asclepiades
about deglutition, appetite, thirst, and excrements, which Caelius
thus depicts:[149] "He says that the first part of deglutition is performed by extension of the fauces; the second by the slenderness of
the passages which lead to the abdomen. Likewise he says that desire
for food, which we have been able to call appetite, that which craves

---

[146] Galen hist. phil. p. 436 T. IV Asclepiades concerning the variety of sperms, like two-
rowed and three-rowed barley

[147] Galen. hist. phil p. 498. Asclepiades says the Aethiopians grow old in sixty years on
account of their bodies being heated by the sun. But those in Britian grow old in a hundred
years on account of the cold For the bodies of the Aethiopians are more relaxed by the sun;
but those of the northern peoples are thicker-skinned.

[148] Sex. Emp adv. Logic I. f 323 p. 433 "For Asclepiades the physician expressly said
that old men lack much of the intelligence and acuteness in comparison with the young; but
in comparison with the false opinions of the majority, the situation was opposite For on account of the many experiences of old men the young considered them deficient in intelligence,
though the situation is opposite For, as I said, old men are much more experienced, though
not more intelligent in comparison with the young."

[149] Cael. Aurel. l.c. p. 44.

food, is due to the greater perfection[150] of passages in the stomach and abdomen. But that which craves drink he says is produced because of small passages. Moreover he denies that excrements of the abdomen (the Greeks say feces) are of a foreign nature. Indeed bodies may even be increased by them. Some animals, finally he says, are solely nourished from them."

[150] Doubtless instead of "greater perfection of passages" should be read "of greater passages", since a little later he explains thirst "because of smaller passages." "Perfection", i.e. size and patency, as Amman warns in the margin at this point.

Chapter VII

CERTAIN PATHOLOGIC AND THERAPEUTIC GENERALITIES

P. 58.   *The Concept of Disease*

Having duly evaluated the concept which Asclepiades formed for himself about the elements of bodies, about the structure and fabric of the healthy body, it will now not be difficult to elicit his concept concerning its diseased state. We know already that he decided that material to be unalterable which could undergo no other change than that deriving from altered connection of the corpuscles. Hence both the material itself can take on itself no pathologic state, but produces disease only in accordance with the abnormal varied composition of its particular elements.[151] (P. 46.) We know also that Asclepiades has proved passages in the animal body, through which, in accordance with their diverse size and form, diverse corpuscles are conducted flowing. If therefore the relation, which subsists between those moving corpuscles and the passages is removed, disease is present. (P. 44. not. 112.)

P. 59.   *Varieties of Diseases*

These postulates having been made, we can now easily perceive what concept Asclepiades has formed for himself of the variety of diseases. For diseases differ according as either the moving corpuscles or the passages assume the cause of the disease. Moving corpuscles produce effects by stasis (by obtrusion of position).[152] But they become static, i.e. their equal flow is intercepted on account of 1) size, 2) figure, 3) number, 4) very rapid motion. But passages are at fault 1) on account of too great size, or 2) on account of too small size, or 3) on account of infrequency. But from what has been stated above we know that, besides flowing corpuscles and passages,

[151] Galen de differ. morb T. III p 199. Introd. p. 375. T. IV. "And the ancient and original elements underlying and constituting the solid bodies consist in nature of this, and, like Erasistratus and Asclepiades, they derive the causes of the diseases therefrom."

[152] Cassius Fel. probl 76. well explains this word: "stasis is mass obstruction by theoretical obstruction on account of wedging."

Asclepiades also postulated a certain tenuous material (spirit), upon which he founded a third class of diseases.[153]

P. 60.   *The Cause of Disease*

As to what concerns the causes of diseases, Asclepiades thinks that humors never constitute the immediate causes of diseases but only the occasions. Hence he also considers that most affections are benefited by plethora, but never produced by it.[154] There still remain in Galen the very words of Asclepiades which he spoke about this matter.[155] "Doubtless Asclepiades thinks, if plethora were the immediate cause of diseases that, when large evacuations were sometimes produced at the beginnings of disease, the result would be that the patient would immediately dispel all detriment and pathology from himself: now, on the contrary, diseases are more often seen themselves to increase, when plethora is purged: as if plethora were the constituent cause of diseases, but in abundant evacuations occurring sometimes at the beginning of the disease, immediately the patient is delivered and gets rid of all disturbances." But now it often appears that the diseases increase as soon as the plethora is purged. Hence Galen says that Asclepiades in these diseases instituted evacuation, not to cure the disease, but to prevent its increase.[156]

P. 61.   *Concerning the Pulse*

Asclepiades says the pulse is a dilation and a contraction of the heart and of the arteries.[157] But he thinks that the heart and the arteries dilate when they are filled with spirit flowing into them through the tenuous covering with which they are equipped inside: when now nothing more flows into their filled lumen, then the tunic

[153] Cael. Aurel. ac. morb. I. 14 p 42: "moreover their stasis is because of either size, or figure, or multitude, or very rapid motion, or bending of the passages, by occlusion, and by expulsion of scales. He says that various effects are produced by differences of places or passages, and not all by stasis of corpuscles, but certain soluble ones by disturbance or turbidity of liquids and of spirit." Galen. Introd p 500 T. IV.

[154] Cael Aurel. l c. p 44 "that the active and effective causes of sickness do not consist in fluids, which they call constituent; but are antecedent, which the Greeks call predisposing: likewise he says that plethora benefits most diseases."

[155] On the contrary, what is said by Julian in Hippoc. aphor. T. V. p. 341?

[156] Galen, Comm. II in Hipp. de natur. hom. p 18. T. V.

[157] Galen. de. differ. puls lib IV. p. 51. T. III. "For Asclepiades himself said that the pulse is a contraction and a dilation of the heart and of the arteries."

returns to its former natural condition.[158] Since he denied all inherent
faculties and powers, it is clear that no power could have produced
the cause of the pulse and its different varieties. Hence Galen warns,
discussing the cause of the strong pulse, that Asclepiades derided
both Herophilus and Athenaeus, who declared the cause of the
strong pulse to be first the strength of the vital function of the arteries, and second the strength of the vital tension; and that the cause
of the strength bore relation to the quantity and tenuity of the
spirit.[159] From these things we can easily conceive how Asclepiades
explained other kinds of pulse. How far his sectarians departed from
him in this, we shall show later.

P. 62.   *Concerning Crises*

We find almost no part of our entire discipline concerning which,
from the times of Hippocrates to the present day, there has been
more discussion on both sides than concerning crises. Even in the
earliest times there were those who were doubtful about these observations of Hippocrates: and especially the Roman physicians in this
matter impugned the reliability of Hippocrates. Among his chief
adversaries emerge our Asclepiades and Celsus, who followed him.[160]
Indeed on this account Asclepiades incurred and underwent many
reproofs, but, as I think, undeservedly. Doubtless because, devoted
to his principles, he could not outline critical days in his doctrine.
But what does Asclepiades deny?—Galen relates that Asclepiades
taught neither that no sudden upsets ever occur in the body of the
patient, nor that very often after them excretions worthy of mention
do not occur: nor that from them a great change is not made in patients, nor that a thing of this sort is not called a crisis: but that when
nature is struggling against the causes producing disease, he tries to
prove that those things should not occur: erring no little in this respect on account of the remarkable masses and passages which he

[158] Galen. de differ. puls. lib. IV. p. 49. T. III: "for this man thinks that both the heart
and the arteries dilate because they are filled with spirit flowing into them through the tenuous material which they have inside themselves; and when they are filled to their former
state, they return again to the condition previously existing by nature in respect to their
tunic."

[159] Galen. de diff. puls. lib. III. p. 55. "the cause of the strength I shall refer to the abundance and tenuousness of spirit."

[160] The classic passage in which Celsus inveighs against crises is III, 4. Whence it is evidently clear that in this matter he took his stand far from the position of Asclepiades. Vid.
Testa. de vitalib. period. To. I. lib. 1. pars 1 c2 P. 7. Foës. Oecoa. Hippocr. s.v. κρίσις.

himself assumed: on account of which he neither knew the powers by which the animal is governed, nor that all these do as much for safety in the well as in the sick; nor because it is they which determine the disease.[161] This classic passage demonstrates amply what Asclepiades denied and what he affirmed.

It is known that Hippocrates, and others vindicating the doctrine of the crisis, have explained it in natural ways, which each adapted to his own principal concepts of vital force. But we know that Asclepiades denied natural force operating on the human body, denied forces and inherent faculties different from the material. Hence also he could not refuse to deny that nature is curative in the diseased state. Therefore he denied, not the thing itself, as Galen well warns, but stated days, which they call critical. For diseases are resolved not at a certain or legitimate time.[162] To these principles he adapted also his method of treatment.

Therefore it is clear in itself that he could not have stood apart from their opinion, in so far as the physician is a minister of nature; and hence he believed that the physician should not await the critical effects of nature, but that the opportunity of time can better be made by art than come of its own accord or by the will of the Gods. Finally he called that the "magnificent" opportunity.[163] Perhaps led by experience, whereby it is known that often excessive forces of nature disturb the crisis and hence render the disease worse, he declared that nature not only helps, but also harms.[164]

P. 63.   *Signs of Diseases*

Caelius Aurelianus[165] reports that the sectarians of Asclepiades decided in accordance with his opinion, that certain of the signs, like a wound of the heart, are pathognomonic of death; and some are not

---

[161] Galen de crisib. lib III. P. 418. T. III. "for Asclepiades could say neither that no sudden upsets ever occur in the body of the patient, nor that they are not often followed by noteworthy excretions, nor that from them a great change is not made in patients, nor that such a thing is not called a crisis· but that when nature is struggling against the causes of disease, he will try to show that these things should not occur, erring far in these things, and on account of the remarkable masses and passages which he assumed. on account of which he did not know the diverse powers of animals, nor that all these things do as much for safety both of the well and of the sick, nor that it is these which decide the disease."

[162] Cael. Aurel. l.c. p. 43.

[163] Cael. Aurel. l.c.

[164] Cael. Aurel. l.c. Cels. III. 4.

[165] Morb. acut. I.1. p. 10.

essential but frequently may be significant, as a wound of the membrane of the head (dura mater), which frequently indicates that the wounded man will die, which frequently, but not invariably and necessarily, occurs.

P. 64.   *The Power of Medicines*

As for what pertains to the power of drugs which they exercise on the human body, some of these, which are stated above, may be inferred by reason. We see here that Asclepiades postulated no specific powers of things. From these things therefore it is already clear that, according to him, drugs could not act by any specific powers.

We see, moreover, that he has declared matter unalterable. It is clear, therefore, that according to his doctrine remedies could have undergone no so-called chemical change. But we see that he declared that the elements of things are corpuscles and passages, and that he placed health in a proper relation of corpuscles and passages, and disease in an impaired relation of them. By right and merit, therefore, it may be gathered that he referred the powers of medicines to this, that they should restore that disturbed relation.[166]

P. 65.   *He Restricts the Use of Medicines*

It is known, from the history of medicine, that all the empirics of that time were engaged in collecting and multiplying a medley of medicines, and that under their auspices a very great number of drugs has already become known. Hence Celsus (*in prooem. ad libr. V. de re med.*) speaks as follows: ".'To these drugs the ancient authors ascribed much, both Erasistratus and those who called themselves Empirics; but especially Herophilus, and those led by him: so that they treated no kind of disease without them."

Celsus continues: "But Asclepiades, not without cause, largely did away with the use of these: and since almost all medicines injure the stomach, and are evil juices, he rather transferred all his own treatment to the regime of living itself."[167] And influenced by these

---

[166] Gal. de simpl. medic. facult. lib. I. p. 5. T. II. Galen relates that some consider that the power whereby medicines act is unknown, and others that it is known, and that others are doubtful among themselves; and that some ascribe it to the warm power, to the cold, to the moist, and to the dry, but others to the corpuscles and the passages. (And some refer it to the size and the shapes and the positions of the corpuscles and pores.) It is clear that Galen knew Asclepiades and his sectarians.

[167] Plin. H.N. XXVI. 3.

things, which I have emphasized as much as possible, there were many who contended that Asclepiades, plainly carried away by zeal of innovation, had condemned the use of all drugs.[168] But let us hear what already Scribon. Larg.[169] has said about this matter. Here he speaks as follows:

Asclepiades said that drugs ought not to be given to the febrile and to those seized with what the Greeks call acute diseases, because he thought they were sometimes safely cured with food and wine suitably given. But in his book, which is inscribed *of preparations*, he contends that "of final resort is a physician who has compositions not for each individual ailment, but for two or three, prepared and tested long before."

P. 66.   *Concerning Emesis*

It was a custom among the Romans, at that time dissolving in luxury and pleasure, that immediately after dinner they should undertake to eject their food by emetic in order that they might then be able to ingest a greater amount.[170] Rightly therefore he condemned vomiting, then excessively frequent.[171] But he did not reject emesis everywhere and completely, which may be seen below in the description of individual diseases: but he avoided it, if he could, lest the stomach should receive any damage thence. Celsus himself says,[172] speaking about emesis and purgation: "he himself also acknowledged that, if there were anything corrupt, it ought to be expelled."

P. 67.   *Concerning Drugs Purging the Bowel*

Asclepiades was primarily offended by the custom of those who held the use of purgations among the luxuries, and approved that they should be used with greater prudence in many diseases. It is established among all that have even tasted doctrine from the lips of ancient physicians that they, influenced by Hippocratic doctrine,

---

[168] Doubtless many have been deceived by the meaning which lurks in the words drug and medicine. For the Greek and Latin writers very often use this word instead of cathartic. Vid. Foef Oec Hipp. s v But it is known that Asclepiades above all others disapproved the use of purgations (P. 67) (vid. Le Clerc. Hist. de Méd. II. 37.).

[169] in epist. ad. Callist.

[170] Concerning this custom of vomiting vid Casaub. ad Suet. Vitell. 13. Rader. ad Mart. lib V. epigr. 75. Ernest. Clav. Cic. Jud Gr. s.v. ἐμέτικα. Concerning drugs, which the ancients used to this end, see Hebenstreft. Palaeol. Therap. p. 588.

[171] Plin. H N. XXVI. 3. Cels. I. 3.

[172] Cels. I. 1.

had decided that there are four fluids in the human body: namely phlegm, yellow bile, black bile, and water.

On this doctrine of the humors they built the power which purgative drugs provided in the bodies of animals. Hence they introduced into their discipline remedies which should expel water (hydragogues), others which should expel yellow bile (cholagogues), others which should expel black bile (melanagogues), and others which should expel phlegm (phlegmagogues). But to explain the reason why various purgations should expel various kinds of humors they employed the varied attractive power inherent in various medicines.

But we know from the things upon which we have commented above concerning the inherent faculties of bodies, according to the opinion of our Asclepiades, that he was little in agreement with those who considered them specific. What wonder, therefore, that, led by the same arguments, he also denied the specific power of purgations, whereby individual ones should expel individual humors from the body. These things having been explained, he was of opinion that the power of cathartic drugs can not be postulated, but that each expels the humor appropriate to itself, so that rather the power of them all should be placed in evacuation alone.

Galen himself suggested a reason, relying upon which Asclepiades would outline the power of purgative drugs in evacuation alone. Doubtless since Asclepiades, relying on those masses and passages and incompact elements, ought to declare that there is in us no quality foreign to nature, so that not even the excrements which daily pass through the bowel are changed; it is evident that, when the bowel is constipated, we are injured by reason of excess, and that the remedy for this is, either to eat less or to refrain altogether from food.[173] Le Clerc[174] thinks that another reason can be found in this contention which Asclepiades makes, that plethora never constitutes an immediate cause of diseases. (P. 60) From these things, therefore, it seems clear that Asclepiades is of opinion that we are not harmed by the acidity, corruption, and putrefaction of things which are in the intestines, but only by their quantity.

[173] Galen de Element. lib. II. p. 58. T. I. "But the masses and passages and incompact elements compel Asclepiades to say the same things. For these are accompanied by the fact that there is no foreign quality of our nature, not even that of the excrements passing through the stomach. But when it leaves the stomach it harms us in the place of the excess; and the treatment is by little food or complete deprivation.

[174] Le Clerc. Hist. de Méd II. 3.7.

But if we proceed a little further in perusing those passages of Galen where he discusses this, we find that Asclepiades thought that not only there is no specific power intrinsic in purgations (cathartics) eductive of individual humors, but rather that these are produced from them. Concerning this subject, Galen drew up a special book, *"de purgant. medicament. facultat."* and there, according to the precepts of the sectarians of Asclepiades, says that every drug in which is the power of purgation converts and transmutes to its own nature whatever humor it touches. For it makes yellow or black bile that which is, as they say, productive of this or that bile: and similarly mucous and aqueous substance, whatever is called by their term productive of phlegm or water.

Finally, the change is of all the humors which are in the veins, not the evacuation of any one, which is called purgation, as their phrase indicates.[175] Which opinion, as I think, Asclepiades doubtless brought forward, induced by the objections of his opponents. Doubtless they opposed him, basing their opinion on weak supports; since, if the power of purgative drugs were located solely in evacuation, the same effect ought to be observed in the treatment of diseases, whether the evacuation of humors were produced by purgation or by venesection. But, to avoid this objection, he declared that at venesection all the humors escaped indifferently; but that when medicine is given, not all but certain ones are selected, and the blood rendered pure.[176]

P. 68.   *Concerning Enemata*

There is very ample use for enemata in the practise of the art; and while the discussion is about them, to what extent and in what way Asclepiades used them, we can assume as the general standard, which he followed, the words Celsus utters:[177] "but generally the bowel

---

[175] Galen de vi medic purg p 484. T. II "The purgative drug, alters whatever fluid it touches into its own form, making yellow bile, which they call a cholagogue, and phlegm, which they call a phlegmagogue; and creating something aqueous by nature, which they call a hydragogue, and demonstrating another which they call black bile, appearing composed of change and modification of all the fluids in the veins, not an evacuation of them all, so-called. Cf. idem de Elem l.c where he tells the same about Asclepiades

[176] Galen de vi medic. purg p 485. "Venesection equally evacuates all the fluids in the veins, but catharsis not equally, but some one and only that of which it is said to be evacuative. Wherefore also they say the blood is purefied by such drugs, not evacuated as in venesections." Concerning this whole matter may be read also Galen de natur. facult I. p. 92. 93. T. I. de Theriac. ad Pison. p. 458. 59. T. II. contr. ea quae a Julian. in Hipp. aph. dict. f. p. 543. T. V.

[177] II. 12.

ought rather to be emptied, which rule by Asclepiades also is so modified that nevertheless it is observed; but I see it is generally passed
over in our century." Likewise:[178] "Asclepiades did away with
medicines, but nevertheless emptied the bowel in almost every disease. But that moderation which he is seen to have followed, is most
appropriate: so that neither is that treatment often tried, and yet,
undertaken once or twice, is not omitted."

But Celsus[179] warns that Asclepiades was in favor of moving the
bowels especially in fevers. Doubtless he thought that fevers arise
from obtrusion of corpuscles occurring in passages: therefore he used
to empty the bowel in fevers, in order that he might dissolve and remove this obstruction. We learn this from Caelius Aurelianus,[180]
when he relates that Asclepiades used enemata in treating phrenitis,
a febrile affection, in order that he might draw off and evacuate the
obtrusion. And on this account, in all diseases with which fever is
associated, Asclepiades had the enema habit, as is clear from the
same Caelius, and below, in a review of the special diseases, we shall
see, unless perchance in these diseases something else should inter-
fere, what might prevent the employment of enemata, as in pleurisy
and pneumonia.[181] Moreover Asclepiades thought that the bowel
ought to be moved when the suspicion is present that acidity is lurking in the intestines: in which cases he counseled injecting enemata
whereby he might remove materials and neutralize them.[182]
Wherefore he also had recourse to enemata for eliminating worms
from the body, as Caelius testifies.[183] But in what cases the use of
enemata is harmful, according to Asclepiades, he reports in these
words: "in all diseases without fevers he judges the use of these substances insidious and troublesome: likewise he judges that weak-
nesses and tremors and severe thirst are specially increased by the
annoyance of injections: "for," he says, "these are destroyers of
strength."[184] But that which Caelius relates of Asclepiades, that
doubtless he forbade the use of enemata in diseases with which no
fever is associated, does not seem always true. For it may be seen

[178] III. 4.
[179] III. 4.
[180] morb. acut. I 15.p. 55.
[181] Cael. Aurel. morb. ac. II. 22. p. 131. II. 29. p. 144.
[182] Cael. Aurel. morb. ac II. 22. p. 131. II. 39. p. 174.
[183] Cael. Aurel. morb. chr. IV. 8. p. 553.
[184] Cael. Aurel. morb. ac. II. 39. p. 174.

from the same Caelius that he counselled moving the bowels in epilepsy.[185] But also our Asclepiades expected a far more striking result from enemata, as Caelius bears witness. Doubtless in the more obstinate diseases, as in tetanus, he injected very strong enemata, in order that he might imitate curative nature and excite a salutary fever.[186]

Celsus discusses admirably the method of moving the bowels according to Asclepiades, and no one will regret reading the actual words of that very agreeable writer.[187] "If the head is heavy, if the eyes are dim, if the disease is of the large intestine, which the Greeks call the colon: if there are pains deep in the abdomen, or in the hip; if some bile runs into the stomach, or even phlegm, or some other fluid like water: if the spirit is restored with difficulty: if the abdomen excretes nothing by itself, but if there are feces and they remain inside: or if the patient perceives the odor of feces from his own gas, though expelling nothing: or if that is putrefied which is expelled: or if the first abstention from food does not dispel the fever: or if the strength does not permit venesection, when there is need, or if the time for it has passed: or if anyone has drunk much before his sickness: or if he who often, either of his own accord or by chance, has been purged, suddenly has a suppression of the bowels. These things are to be avoided: not to move the bowels before the third day, that no acidity remain either in the weak body long exhausted by ill health or in that in which the bowel moves sufficiently every day, or which has a liquid movement, nor at the onset itself of an attack; because what is then injected is retained in the abdomen and carried back into the head and makes the danger much more severe. But on the previous day, the patient ought to fast, so that he may be fit for such treatment. And some hours before, on the same day, he ought to drink warm water, so that his upper parts may be moist, and then move his bowels with a pure, fresh, water enema, if we are satisfied with a mild medicine.

But if we want it a little stronger, let it be mixed with honey: but if mild, let it be made from water in which the herb fenugreek, or

[185] Cael. Aurel. morb. chr. I. 4. p. 321.

[186] Cael. Aurel. morb. ac. III 8 p. 215. Cf. Bianchini la med. d'Ascl. disc. II. P. VII.

[187] Almost all these words of Celsus are referable to Asclepiades, and beyond doubt are taken from his book which he wrote about enemata (vid. cap. III) as Bianchini has already suspected. I.i.

barley, or mallow has been boiled. If for the purpose of checking movement, from verbenas. But sea-water is sharp, or any to which salt has been added, and both are better and more suitable when boiled. It would be sharper if either oil or saltpetre were added, or also honey. If it is sharper, it expels so much the more, but is less easily tolerated. That which is injected should be neither cold nor hot, lest in either case it do harm. When there has been injected as much as possible, the patient should remain in bed, nor yield immediately to the first desire of dejection. When it is necessary, let him sit down. And in this way material removed from the upper parts of the body takes the disease with it. But when, sitting down as often as is necessary, anyone becomes exhausted, he ought to lie quiet for a while; and, lest his strength fail, let him take some food that day: and he should be given more or less, by reason of that attack, which will be expected, and ought to be so considered lest he should be in fear."

P. 69.   *Concerning Venesection*

Galen relates that Asclepiades employed venesection, although he was so eager for contention that he criticized almost all doctrines of doctors and spared no one of the previous century, not even Hippocrates; and so did not hesitate to call the ancients' method of treatment a meditation of death.[188]

From these things, therefore, we have ascertained that Asclepiades employed venesection, but did not use it promiscuously, but rather circumscribed it by certain suitable limits of doctrine, which he taught. Doubtless by incision, which is made in a vein, blood is evacuated. But according to him blood consists of larger corpuscles, as we have already shown in a previous discussion. Hence also in the diseased state, then only the evacuation of blood can take place through the divided vein, if the larger corpuscles are affected: which indeed suffer in all diseases with which pains are associated.[189] But nevertheless, if blood is evacuated in those diseases which do not permit venesection, the blood seems to escape thin, clear, and dilute.[190]

[188] Galen. de Ven sect adv. Erasistr. p. 3. T. IV
[189] Cael. Aurel morb acut. I. 15 p. 46.
[190] Cael. Aurel. morb acut. II. 29 p 143. The statements are obscure which Asclepiades outlined concerning section of a vein in diseases combined with severe pains, since in every disease the patient is beset with pains. It is evident, therefore, that he understood certain

Although Asclepiades is of opinion that no other disabilities of the body can be mitigated by venesection except those which arise from the blood, he employs it also for lessening the force of the blood and diminishing difficulty of breathing,[191] as for evacuating plethora, which is chiefly present in the veins.[192]

Asclepiades also warns that, in instituting the venesection, account is especially to be taken of the regions in which patients reside: he testifies that he has observed that to pleuritics venesection brings no benefit at Rome and at Athens, but that rather it brings harm; whereas in the Hellespont and at Parium, they are truly restored by it.[193] Although Asclepiades is severely rebuked on this account by Caelius, nevertheless this can be vindicated by the soundest arguments. For we know how important for changing the course of diseases are weather, kind of life, regime of living, and other things of this sort, which the physician ought to consider in his treatment of diseases: we know that cities, which abound in a numerous quantity of inhabitants, in which luxury, lust, and other vices thrive, are more prone to convert diseases to the gastric and putrefactive state.

Le Clerc[194] is in error, in stating that Asclepiades never counselled venesection in fevers. At any rate he used to do it in those fevers in which, according to the principles of his doctrine, he thought that benefit would redound to his patients from it.[195] Then, indeed, venesection should be employed at the very height of the fever: "for," says he, "the removal of corpuscles can become difficult

---

peculiar and particular pains which, if they should afflict the body, would require venesection. and, unless I am entirely mistaken, Asclepiades doubtless meant to denote inflammatory pains. For Galen (de meth. med. lib. XIII p. 173 To. IV infra cap VIII) reports that Asclepiades, equally with other physicians, explains inflammation by the blood flowing in an unnatural way to a certain part of the body, there stagnating in the smallest veins, and forming a tumor. But from those passages for which we have praised Caelius, we perceive this, that Asclepiades urged venesection in those diseases in which blood (larger corpuscles) is affected. Thence it is also clear how Asclepiades was led to be able to declare, in those diseases in which venesection really does not have a place, if nevertheless it is instituted, the blood escapes thin, clear, and dilute. For in the inflammatory state, the blood is thicker and more prone to coagulation. Nor can he instil this scruple into us that, according to Asclepiades, the cause of pain lurks in the most minute corpuscles (p 48. not. 126.). For we also evacuate blood in inflammatory pains, although we have placed the seat of pain in the nerves

[191] Cael. Aurel. morb chr. II. 13 p. 416.
[192] Cael. Aurel. morb. ac. III. 9. 216.
[193] Cael. Aurel. morb acut. II. 22. p. 131.
[194] Le Clerc. Hist. de méd II. 3.7.
[195] Cael. Aurel. morb. ac. III. 4. p. 193. infra Cap. VIII.

at the time of remission."[196] He was accustomed to institute venesection in the most diverse parts of the body; either in the foot,[197]
or in the arm, or in the forehead, or at the angles of the eyes, or in the
veins which are under the tongue.[198] And he used to use cupping-
glasses, which he recommended should be employed only when
neither fevers should prevent the removal of material, nor plethora
should be present in the veins, nor there should be some major cause
which, by contrary force should overcome the force of the cupping-
glass, so that he could not accomplish removal.[199] Doubtless in
fevers he ought to advise against cupping-glasses, on account of the
greater obtrusion of corpuscles than can be overcome by the power of
cupping-glasses.

P. 70.   *The Gymnastic Art*

Asclepiades was the first of the Greek physicians practising their
art in Rome who suggested that the various methods of exercising
and restoring the body, which are universally wont to be enumerated
in the gymnastic art, are also useful in treating disease.

We have ascertained from the history of our art that even before
Hippocrates there was a certain Herodicus,* who both himself restored his own lost health by walking, and, on account of good success in this, devoted a part of all medicine to the universal gymnastic
art. Whence it was employed by Greek physicians, not only for preserving health, but also for dispelling diseases, and there was argument about its use in various ways: some flatly rejected it, others
extolled it to the stars: some maintained that it should be used only
for preserving health: others restricted its limits to the treatment of
diseases.

It is known to everyone that, after Greece was conquered, the Romans were themselves made Greeks when, by wealth and resources
transported to Rome, they established there both corrupt morals,
luxury, lust, and a more delicate and effeminate abode and manner

[196] Cael. Aurel. morb. ac. III. 8. p. 216. Celsus (III.18) states the opposite about Asclepiades, who in remission counselled venesection.

[197] Cael. Aurel. morb. acut. I. 14. p. 44. "Similarly beneficial to this he says is removal of
blood done from the ankle, from its medial or posterior tibial vein or great saphenous vein.

[198] Cael. Aurel. morb. acut. III. 4 p. 193.

[199] Cael. Aurel morb. acut. III. 8. p 217. III. 4 p. 193.

* A celebrated physician of Selymbria in Thrace, who was a tutor and predecessor of
Hipprocates in the 5th century B.C.

of living. In the times of Asclepiades, the Romans had already reached almost the highest peak of softness and luxurious living, and indulged in pleasures from day to day. They used baths and everything which could make them soft, arts devised with the utmost delicacy of mind, massage, ointments. They contrived various ways of moving the body gently, transportations in the saddle, riding in a litter; they had travelling by chariot, and journeys by ship most elegant in delights. (Chap. IV). What wonder, therefore, that the Romans had a highly popular physician, who permitted the use of this manner of living even in diseases? This physician was our Asclepiades, who, by these arts, knew how to make the hateful Greek medicine acceptable and popular to the Romans.[200] He was most celebrated on account of this dietetic portion combined with his medicine; and indeed it is to be regretted that his scribes have left us so little about his method, which he had made his own, and this little so uncertain. No doubt greater light might be shed on his doctrine, and assuredly advantage would redound to us therefrom. For it cannot be denied that in our times also the method of treatment would receive great benefit from a more judicious use of this dietetics, and as much as possible it is to be regretted that very clearly this has been exiled from our medicine.[201]

Asclepiades followed Erasistratus in that he maintained that exercises conduce nothing to healthy bodies.[202]

This seems altogether remarkable, and the scribes do not furnish the reasons which induced him to forbid these things to the healthy, but commend them to the sick. Perhaps he wished to restrict their too celebrated use to the Romans? Perhaps he really thought this up relying on the arguments which Mercurialis[203] brings forward, which I do not remember reading anywhere in the writings of the ancients as Asclepiadean.

But, lest we should seem to be too tedious in our preliminary statements, we now intend to investigate everything which Asclepiades proposed concerning the gymnastic art.

[200] Plin. H N. XXV. 3 "and when everyone understood this, that he could surpass himself, if everything were favorable, that those things were true which were easiest, he converted almost the whole human race to himself, in no other way than if he had come sent down from heaven."

[201] Bianchini: la med. d'Asclep. disc. III. P. I–IV.

[202] Galen. de tuend. valet. I. p. 225. To. I.

[203] de art. gymn. IV. 2. p. 250.

P. 71.   I. *Concerning Massage*[204]

"But concerning massage and transportation he wrote as much as the inventor thereof: but in that volume which he wrote of the common aids, although he made mention of only three, of this and of horse and of litter transportation, yet he devoted the greatest part to massage. But in this we ought not to belittle more recent men, either what they discovered or rightly followed; and all those things which are found among some of the elders ought to be credited to their authors. And it cannot be doubted that Asclepiades taught more widely and more clearly when and how massage should be employed, though he discovered nothing which was not comprehended by the oldest author, Hippocrates, in a few words."[205]

Massage differs in accordance with various methods of rubbing, is either vigorous or gentle, much or moderate, longer or shorter. It differs again in accordance with various accessories with which the body is rubbed, either with the hands alone, cold or warm, or with cloths, or with oil, or with ointments: it differs also in accordance with the various parts of the body which are rubbed.

Asclepiades used these various methods of rubbing the body in order that he might dispel from it various ailments, and he seems to have followed Hippocrates, who said[206] by massage, if it is vigorous, the body is hardened: if gentle, it is softened: if much, it is reduced: if moderate, it is filled out. So in pains of the intestines, he says, the parts which are suffering ought to be rubbed with oil, a long time, and industriously, as much as the places themselves can tolerate.[207] To the vigorous massage, which he uses, belong also those which are with retained spirit, and in which he thought to dispel water in dropsy[208] —By that gentle tickling, by which the skin is softened with mild friction, so that he did not even apply forcibly the hand which was rubbing, he thought he should bring it about that sleep would ensue[209]—To dispel the frigid torpor by which the body had been seized, he advised to massage with warm hands and to wrap the parts in cloths[210]—For convulsions he rubs all the spines of the

[204] Bianchini disc. III. P. IV.
[205] Cels. II. 24.
[206] Cels. l.c.
[207] Cael. Aur morb. ac. III. 17. p. 245.
[208] Cael. Aur. morb. chr. III. 8. p. 489.
[209] Cels. III. 18.
[210] Cael. Aur. morb. ac. II. 39. p. 176.

vertebral column day and night continually, no doubt with this intention, to dispel spasms.[211]

In fever massage is not useful except in its remission.

From these things, therefore, which we have related[212] with the greatest possible delight, it is evidently clear that Asclepiades employed massage to dispel and remove stagnant fluids, to open the pores, to induce sleep, to soften and warm the parts. It will be a more appropriate place to understand this in the description of diseases to which he applied the method of massage.

P. 72.   II. *Concerning Transportation*

Of all the exercises which have been devised for the treatment of diseases, assuredly the easiest, and by far the most convenient, is transportation, which the patient can use, even if he is so infirm that he cannot move himself. He can be busy in the fields, outdoors, enjoy the sunshine, be restored by fresh air: he can be moved in a quiet and pleasant way, as long as he pleases.[213]

"But several kinds of transportation are available: which are in accordance both with the strength and with the means of the patient, that they may not be too fatiguing for the weakest nor too expensive for the lowly. The gentlest of transportations is by boat, either in harbor or on a river: more strenuous in a ship on the deep sea, or by litter or bench: rougher by vehicle. And these themselves can be lessened and mitigated."[214] Most physicians think transportation is not to be employed except in the remission of fever, and in terminal disease. But Asclepiades says it should be used also in recent and severe and burning fever, and especially for dispelling it.[215]

The effect which transportation exerts on the body is this, that the passages are made more open.[216] Doubtless fever arises, according to Asclepiades, from obstruction of the pores and impeded removal of the corpuscles (infra Chap. VIII). Therefore, in order to treat it, he devised remedies which should dissolve the stagnations and restore the interrupted flow of corpuscles; and to this end especially he designated transportation, which, by its gentle, passive

[211] Cael. Aur morb ac III. 8. p. 216.
[212] Bianchini disc. III. P. V.
[213] Bianchini disc III. P. V.
[214] Cels. II. 15 Merc. de art. gymn III, 10. sqq Gesn in Christ Plin. XC. not. 9.
[215] Cels. l.c.
[216] Cael. Aurel. morb. ac. I. 15. p. 55.

motion removes obstructions, impels the lagging corpuscles, and re-
stores their removal. Hence we can also understand what it is, moved
by which Asclepiades praised transportation in recent and severe
fever, and especially in dispelling burning fever.

But lest the removal of corpuscles should be too much increased
by transportation, and thence the patients would become deficient,
he thinks transportation should be employed rather by night and
after food.[217] Doubtless by night, that is, after dinner: but after
that, since corpuscles, eliminated from the body by the movement of
transportation, are restored in foods, dissolved in the stomach, to the
corpuscles, which then are carried through the whole body.

Then he thought that transportation serves also by giving abundant sleep. Hence in treating phrenitis, he says, sufficient motion for
giving adequate rest will be employed with a sedan chair, because it
soon makes the sick soft and delicate.[218] In hemoptysis he forbids
transportation, lest the loss of blood be thereby increased.[219]

P. 73.   III. *Hanging Couches*

Mercurialis thinks that these were attached at their four corners
by ropes to the roofs of beds in such a way that they are raised a
little from the ground, as if they seemed to be hanging in the air.[220]
Celsus informs us of the twofold way of using them: the couch ought
either to be suspended and moved, or at least a small rope placed
under one foot of the bed, and so the couch moved this way and that
by hand.[221]

The effect, for the sake of which Asclepiades used hanging couches,
was no other than what we have already seen derive from transportation. Hence Pliny says:[222] he also devised other comforts by also
suspending couches, by whose swaying he either mitigated diseases
or allured sleep.

[217] Cael. Aurel. morb. ac. l.c. p. 52.
[218] Cael. Aurel. l c.
[219] Cael. Aurel. Morb. chr. II. 13 p. 417.
[220] de art. gym. VI. ii. et III. c. 12.
[221] Cels. l.c. others prefer to read "a prop should be placed under one foot of the bed,"
and this reading is more attractive. For the couch can more easily and better be moved this
way and that with a prop placed underneath than if it stands on the earth floor, ground, or
pavement.
[222] Plin. H.N. XXVI. 3.

P. 74.   *IV. Concerning Perambulation*

Few and imperfect are the things which are read in the writings of the ancients about this aid and adjunct of Asclepiades. There is no doubt that he taught the same things which are found in the writings of the methodic sect about this famous and admirable method, or even that he was chief author of them.[223] But in such a deficiency of witnesses, we do not know what things are really due to Asclepiades. Hence we can relate here only those things which are found in writers as certain doctrines of Asclepiades.

But already, from those things which we have related thus far, we see that all the ancients have been in this field of therapeutic medicine; and this is proved also by the diligence which they employed in perambulations. Not only they urged this, that they should move the body in perpetual perambulation; but rather this also, that they should exercise and refresh the body by various methods of perambulations, in various ways, both gently and violently. They always had an excellent reason, either for the motion itself, or the place in which the ambulatory exercises are performed, or the time in which and for how long they are done.[224] Asclepiades uses walking and running most, in order to disperse and eliminate fluids collected in certain parts of the body, as in dropsy. He uses perambulation in sandy places, to strengthen relaxed parts.[225] Caelius also makes mention of some other perambulation which Asclepiades employed to oppose too great laxity of the parts, and calls it the contest or climbing of the woods.[226]

[223] The writings of Caelius Aurelianus, Aretaeus, and others who have discoursed on this subject, deserve to be read again and again to this end Excellently and more fully, Prosperus Alpinus has written about "methodic medicine," and Mercurialis about "the gymnastic art." vid. Bianchini disc. III. P. VI.

[224] Cael Aurel. morb. chr. III. 8. p. 489.

[225] Cael. Aurel. morb. chr. II. 1. p. 364. From other comments of ancient authors also we have ascertained that such perambulations have been used in the sand, for restoring lost strength to the parts. So Augustus, when he was suffering with his left hip, thigh, and leg, was strengthened by this perambulation. Vid. Suet Aug c 80. From this it is more than sufficiently clear that not weakness of muscles is to be understood, but that which is in nerves. Hence Asclepiades used perambulation in sand for the paralysis, and Augustus was freed from his sciatic pain. In these diseases more recent authors use the sand bath with good success.

[226] The scamma, or contest, (according to Almeloveen. not. ad h. 1 p. 64. o.) is when patients placed across a machine made from metal and wooden materials, like a rack, were ordered to rise above the thwarts by agitation of the body and their own effort. Amman. ad

P. 75.   V. *About Baths*

It is established among all that about the age of Asclepiades the use of baths by the Romans became so celebrated that they lived in them a great part of the day: no wonder, therefore, that our Bithynian, with them, advised using them in the treatment of diseases, having acquired so many sectarians and partisans who with the greatest pleasure adopted his doctrines and put them into use.[227]

Assuredly it is to be regretted that we leave the ancients very poor in respect to the use which Asclepiades had made his own. Although it is not improbable that many things, which are read in the writings of the methodics, were taught by Asclepiades himself: nevertheless nothing certain can be declared, what and how many of them are due to him.[228]

Celsus reports a double use of the baths: "For he makes a beginning of more food and of stronger wine with health in the fevers discussed: it only removes the fever and is always employed when it hastens the relaxation of the surface skin, and the elicitation of corrupt fluid, and a change in the habit of the body. The ancients used to use it too timidly, Asclepiades uses it more boldly. And this circumstance ought not to terrify, if it is timely: but prematurely, it does harm."[229]

P. 76.   VI. *Hanging Baths*

Hanging baths, first invented by Sergius Orata, who lived about the age of Asclepiades,[230] and first used by Asclepiades in dispelling diseases,[231] are not unworthy to be mentioned here briefly. There is conflict concerning them, their manufacture and structure, among learned men. Gesner[232] thinks they were constructed in a so-called hypocaust, or vaulted chamber warmed from below, under which a kindled fire with its flame could lick and warm the base and sides of

---

h i. thinks it is the end of the space which those leap across who exercise themselves by leaping, either made with a long pole applied, or by drawing a furrow. Vid. Th Reines. Var. Lect. III. 18, p 166 and Lexic Goelian s v.

[227] Plin. H N XXVI. 3 "already men constructed baths with the most eager desire, and many other things, welcome and pleasant to be mentioned."

[228] See Bianchini disc. III. P. VII. Prosp. Alpin de medic. method. lib. V. Cap. VII.

[229] Cels II. 17.

[230] Plin. H N. IX. c. 54.

[231] Plin. H.N XXVI 3. "infinite soothing being imparted for the first time by a hanging bath."

[232] Gesn. in Christ. Plin. XC. not. 22.

the bath: and that the water was conducted through various tubes and in these was warmed in varying degree, so that, on being let down from a height, it would descend into the bath either warm, or tepid, or cold, according to the pleasure of the bather. This opinion is based on an ancient carved monument (*in Fabric. ad Sext. Emp. p. 30.*)

But Mercurialis thinks[233] that hanging baths were not those made on roofs or vaulted chambers as they wished, but were nothing else than those troughs of marble or bronze or wood attached to ceilings in imitation of couches, whereby, with the slightest impulse of the hands, they could be agitated either gently or vigorously. Therefore he has persuaded himself that whatever physicians prescribed exercise with these motions had this one thing particularly in mind, to produce motion without labor or any fatigue: then that they took care lest, in that exercise any pleasure should be lacking, which forsooth would be found great in couches, but greatest in baths, which, besides that sweetest motion, would add the delectation of water, while they touched individual members of the body with the softest and gentlest caress. Mercurialis then continues: "if hanging baths are understood to have been those which were built above roofs, I do not see how in them that pleasure on account of which, according to Seneca and Pliny, they were devised, would be found greater than in others. But in that case does not the same pleasure arise of water conducted from a height? Then it does not seem probable that those great troughs filled with water, would have been hung from ceilings: and that monument depicted in Fabricius seems to remove all doubt.

Concerning the advantage, benefit, and use which Asclepiades expected from these hanging baths employed in the treatment of diseases, the writers make no report. But it is not difficult to be perceived that the effects were fully produced which we have described from baths, from transportation and from hanging couches.[234]

P. 77. VII. *Cold Baths*

Asclepiades is surely above all praise as the first author to describe the medical use of cold water with such favor that he would

---

[233] Mercur. de art. gymn. III. 12. 232.

[234] So Bianchini disc. III P. IX. provokingly says of the structure of baths according to the opinion of Mercurialis: "The first attests only to the refinement of pleasure, rendering the water agreeably mobile in the act of bathing: the second seeks to unite in a single act the virtue of the bath and that of transportation."

be proud to be named from it.[235] The ancients relate nothing which can inform us about the things which he taught: but no doubt his doctrines were very famous, which his sectarians embraced with so much enthusiasm, methodists and pneumatists, and which to the present day are vindicated by physicians in every way.[236]

Not only did he advise bathing in cold water, but he spoke also about its internal use. "It is extremely useful," he says, "to drink water, both to bathe in it cold, which they call cold-bathing, and to drink it cold.[237]

So in diarrhoea, even that accompanied by colic, fever, and gripes, Asclepiades declared, contrary to previous authors, that there ought to be assiduous drinking of cold water, and indeed as cold as possible.[238]

But let us not believe that Asclepiades promiscuously and without using any discretion recommended the drinking of cold water, relates Celsus, or that he may be judged, by those coming from the bath and sweating, that it was useless.[239]

P. 78.   VIII. *Compression of the Respiration*

Galen reminds us that compression of the respiration between exercises, and especially between apotherapeutic exercises, has been restored by the best gymnasts.[240] It is performed when exhalation is checked while all the muscles seen about the ribs are tense and contracted.[241] The compression of respiration which physicians employ is twofold: if either the muscles of the thorax are tense, while those in the diaphragm and abdomen are relaxed, so that the excrements are more easily thrust downward, or these muscles also are tense, so that those viscera also which are under the diaphragm ex-

[235] Plin. H.N. XXVI. 3. "he himself preferred to be named or known for giving or using cold water, on the authority of M. Varro." Hence Haeduinus gathers from this passage that Asclepiades was called Dosipsychron or, as Gesnerus in Christ. Plin. Conjectures, Psychrodotes, in imitation of cold bath, from which psychrolytes is named.

[236] Cael. Aurel. morb. acut. I. 14. p. 44.

[237] Some things are related below concerning the use of cold water, cap. VIII, where the discussion is about hydrophobia. Cf. Plin. H.N. XXV. P. 38. Dio. Cass. lib. LIII, Cap. 30. Concerning Cassius, a sectarian of Asclepiades, vid. Cels. in introd. Cf. Prosp. Alpin. de medic. method lib. V. cap. 7. Bianchini disc. III. P. VIII.

[238] Cels. IV. 91.

[239] Cels. I. 3. Cf. Bianchini disc. II. P. XIII.

[240] Galen. de tuend. valet. lib. III. p. 245. T. IV.

[241] Galen l.c.: "when all the muscles of the thorax are tense and those of the pleura extended, we compress the respiration."

perience the beneficial result of the exercise. But always both the thorax and the abdomen are girded with certain sheaths whereby the exercise succeeds more easily and happily. The effect, which thence results to the body, is that the excrements, which lurk in the thorax and the abdomen, are eliminated and the animal heat is increased.[242]

Whether Asclepiades himself used compression of the respiration in place of aid and medicine, we do not know, since the writers mention nothing of this sort. But Galen reports that he declared it harmful because the head is thereby congested.[243] This was well observed by Asclepiades and is confirmed by daily experience. Doubtless, if breathing is impeded, the reflux of blood from the head is intercepted, wherefrom it results that the head is congested by its abundance, the veins and arteries are distended, the eyes swell, the face reddens, and there is little short of the apoplectic state arising.

P. 79.   *Wine and its Medical Use*

Wine, and the use which Asclepiades had made of it in dispelling diseases, belong prominently to those things on account of which his method of treatment was particularly distinguished, though disliked with many disparagements and rebukes. Caelius Aurelianus moves every stone on this account to disparage the illustrious name of Asclepiades. But whoever reads a little more accurately what we find outlined in Caelius cannot deny that Asclepiades, when he discourses about administering wine to the sick, is worthy of being numbered among the most eminent men of our art. Therefore we shall seem to be doing something worth while when we vindicate and rescue from the medley of disparagements those few data which have come down to us.

Hence he numbers wine among the common aids[244] in that book which he had written about first aids, and makes mention of it more often in his book about "Administration of Wine." (See above, Chap. III.) In his book about common aids he said that wine is of both properties. "For," he says, "just as curds thicken and thin the nature of milk when cheese is curdled from milk and a thinner and more liquid material is made from it, and modified by the same prop-

[242] Mercurial. de. art. gymn. III. 6. p. 203 sq. VI. 4. p. 353.
[243] Galen. l.c. p. 247.
[244] Plin. H.N. XXVI III.3.

erty these opposites are separated; not otherwise also wine; by a certain power of its impact, makes us receive a larger portion of nourishment to thicken, but collect more to dissolve and make thin and extenuate."[245]

Caelius pours out derision on this account; but who does not know that milk mixed with wine turns to curds? Doubtless, taught by this experience, Asclepiades thinks that nutritive fluid mixed with wine experiences the same fortune. But assuredly Asclepiades did not think in a word to approve the use of wine by this property, which he considered dangerous in the treatment of phrenitis: he related in his books about common aids this experiment instituted for the purpose of exploring the properties of wine, as the physiologic truth based on experience and use. But Caelius, to oppose Asclepiades that it is dangerous to drink wine in phrenitis, repeats this experience with the purpose of proving that Asclepiades has contradicted himself. But for what reason he gave wine in dangerous phrenitis we shall see a little later, when it is clear that he did well to have advised treatment with this medicine for patients impaired by a phrenitis.

Cael. (I. I.) continues in these words: "Asclepiades says that the drinking of wine is safer in chronic affections than in acute ones; and in those which are relieved by remissions more than in those which afflict by their continuity; and in the aged more than in the young; and in those who have been purged beforehand, by enema, or who are thirsty, more than those who are full of food; and in incipient or abating fevers more than in those at their height; and after an accession, rather than before it." Is anyone not overwhelmed with supreme joy, reading such precepts? Is not the name rightly and deservedly due to Asclepiades of physician flourishing with admirable judgment, judging with superlative genius all things pertaining to the exercise of the art? Is it not in our times also the greatest honor and adornment to a physician, that, in applying remedies, he should have regard to those considerations which do not permit their promiscuous use? and Asclepiades appears conspicuously adorned by these virtues. He praises wine and administers it to the sick, but does not employ it promiscuously, led by empiric knowledge or blinded by the authority of others: he is well able to distinguish those

[245] Cael. Aurel. morb. acut. I 25. p. 58.

things which counsel its use from those which prohibit it. He considers the disease itself, he considers its time and state, he considers ages and other things which pertain thereto.

Now the question arises, moved by what reasons and considerations, and in what diseases, did Asclepiades exhibit wine, and what did he think are the hidden powers in it? In the first place, many diseases, whose treatment Caelius reports, teach us that Asclepiades thought the use of wine effective for removing weakness and laxity, and for restoring the strength to convalescents exhausted by disease.[246] It concerns this also that he believed that the dormant strength of life is stimulated by wine.[247] But that, which all who thus far have treated the history of Asclepiades have chiefly taken amiss, is that they are completely persuaded that he also gave wine to the febrile. But with all the diligence which is possible I have re-read those passages by which they seemed to be supported, but have found nothing by which I could be moved to add pebbles to their opinion. Therefore it is worth while that we should consider a little about those passages. At any rate, it is true that Caelius Aurelianus relates that Asclepiades ordered wine to be given to the febrile, but he himself also warns that he gave it "with added discretion."[248]

Doubtless almost always he used to recommend wine at the end of fevers for restoring and stimulating exhausted strength. This is proved by the passages sought from Caelius which we have chiefly mentioned, to which it is a pleasure to add Celsus.[249] But when he administered wine in the treatment of pernicious phrenitis and cardiac disease, doubtless he did nothing else than what is confirmed also by our method of treatment, namely, that in the suppurative or nervous stage of diseases no remedy is superior to wine. He was accustomed to allow wine to patients affected with stupor, but not so much that fever was produced by the medicine as that rather he thought it would dispel the lethargy. A more opportune place for discussing these things will be below, under Chap. VIII.

As we peruse the writings of the ancients we encounter various kinds of wines, which either by nature itself were different, or were

---

[246] Cael Aurel morb. acut I. 15. p. 49 morb acut. II. 22 p. 132. morb. acut. III. 21, p. 263 morb. chr. II i p. 365 morb. chr II. 7 p 386. Cels. III 21.

[247] Cael Aurel. morb. ac II. 9. p. 87

[248] Cael Aurel. morb. ac. I. 14. p. 43.

[249] Cels. III. 14.

so conditioned by art, that they clearly assumed another nature. This varied nature of wines Asclepiades used always to respect, and did not think the wine was the same, whatever it was which he advised for patients.—It is known to everyone who has even only approached the threshholds of old monuments how soberly and temperately the ancients behaved in respect to the daily and customary use of wine. For they were almost always accustomed to drink wine so mixed with water that the greatest part of the mixture would be water. What wonder, therefore, that the old doctors allowed the sick a freer and larger use of wine, so that they did not forbid it even to the febrile.[250]

Asclepiades also used to comply with this custom, that he should administer that wine for the greatest part diluted and mixed with water. But sometimes he was accustomed to change the proportion of wine and water. Thus in catarrh he so tempered the wine that he mixed one cup of wine with one of water, so that the quantity of wine and of water were equal.[251] In heart disease he orders pure wine to be given unmixed,[252] thinking doubtless that there is greater power of constricting and strengthening in pure wine. But as he was accustomed to respect the varying method of tempering the wine, so also he used to think it was sometimes appropriate to add other things for medicinal purpose. So we read that according to the accustomed manner of the ancients he ordered salt water to be mixed with the wine, a kind of artificial beverage which is called brine wine. Doubtless he had persuaded himself that from added salt water wine acquires a greater power of stimulating, strengthening, and constricting, and flows more quickly to all parts of the body.[253] That kind of wine also, which was called mulled, he used to administer often to the sick.[254] To this mulled wine sometimes he used to add also other things, like rue and hyssop or barley.[255]

In the same way also he used to consider differences which are in wines from their native soil. So Caelius Aurelianus warns that he gave Samothracian wine[256] to those suffering from tropical fever. In

[250] See Mercurial. Var. Lect. lib. I. cap. 16 and Le Clerc. Hist. de Méd. II. 5.7.
[251] Cael. Aur. morb. chr. II. 7. p. 386.
[252] Cael. Aur. morb. ac. II. 39. p. 176.
[253] Cael. Aurel. morb. acut. I. 15. p. 55. morb. ac. II. 39. p. 175.
[254] Cael. morb. ac. I. 15. p. 51. de mulsi. confect. vid. Oribas. collect. medic.
[255] Cael Aurel. morb. ac. II. 22. p. 130. morb. ac. III. 21. p. 263.
[256] Cael. Aurel. morb. ac. I. 14. p. 43.

respect to the quantity of wine which he exhibited, or the time of giving it, he was accustomed always to consider the nature both of the wine and of the patient, the time and stage of the disease, or its character, and in general everything which is wont to be associated with these phenomena. So in intermittent fever he orders to drink[257] half a pint, a greater quantity for lethargics than for phrenetics,[258] night and day, and continuously in heart disease.[259] But the best time, which he thought most suitable for giving wine, is the end of diseases, as we have already shown, especially of fevers. He approves also giving wine after food: for if it is given alone it will easily penetrate, and go through bodies, not otherwise than as if, without any dregs it were poured through sieves, whose cavities, if nothing interferes, easily receive it, and return what has been received. But if it is given after food, he says, it will remain, not otherwise than as if, as was said above, it were poured into sieves with the dregs.[260]

These are the things which we have thought worth while to bring forward concerning the way in which Asclepiades used wine in overcoming diseases. From these things it is clearly obvious that it added great praise to him, as if he had said that the usefulness of wine could scarcely be equalled by the power of the gods,[261] that he perceived well and admirably its various powers, and that it ought to be counted among the greatest powers in our art on account of the use which he made of it in the treatment of diseases. Already among the older physicians a certain Cleophantus had illustrated the rationale of wine, whose precepts in general Asclepiades had so followed that he seemed to be rather the author of the precepts.[262] Hence Apuleius says: "he was also the first to discover that the sick are benefited by wine, but forsooth by giving it in time, in the observance of which he was very skilful."[263]

P. 80. *The Use of Music in Treatment of Diseases*

There was and is contention among physicians whether any power is to be ascribed to music in the treatment of diseases, and no less

[257] Cael. Aurel. morb. ac. I. 14. p. 43.
[258] Cael. Aurel. morb. ac. II. 9. p. 87.
[259] Cael. Aurel. morb. ac. II. 39. p. 176.
[260] Cael. Aurel. morb. ac. II. 39. p. 176.
[261] Plin. H.N. XXIII. 22.
[262] Plin. H.N. XXVI. 3.
[263] Apuleius in Florid. IV. p. 276. cf. Plin. H.N. VII. 37.

dispute as to what it may be. There are those who plainly deny its power: there are those who affirm it, and Asclepiades dissents from their opinion, some of whose motives are extant in authors from whom in a way it may be gathered what benefit he imagined the diseased body might take therefrom.[264]

So far as is clear from what the writers relate, the chief value of music, according to the opinion of Asclepiades, is to be found in those diseases in which the mind is affected. Hence the minds of phrenitics, disturbed by disease, are often restored to their own nature by a symphony.[265] In the same way he teaches that a song should be employed in the treatment of mania. Caelius speaks thus to many according to his opinion: "they use also madrigals of pipes with varied modulations: one of these they call the Phrygian mode, which is gay and excites those known to be insane from sorrow: another is serious, which they call the Doric mode, or which, by occupying the mind, counsels shame, injecting sternness, as in war, in those who are affected with laughter or childish giggling."[266] To this pertains the treatment of phrenitis, which Celsus admirably describes with the same understanding as Asclepiades, speaking thus: "but it is necessary to act contrary to the minds of those thus insane, according to the nature of each. For the vain fears of some must be relieved; as happens in a very rich man fearing hunger to whom false inheritances were reported. And of some the boldness must be restrained, as is done in those in restraining whom blows also are employed. Of some also the untimely laughter must be prevented by scolding and threats. And of some the sad thoughts should be dispersed: for which symphonies, and cymbals, and noise are beneficial."[267]

---

[264] See Bianchini disc. III. P.x. Roger. tent. de vi soni et musices in corp. hum. (Aven 1758) P. 251. p. 99

[265] Censorin. de die natal. cap. 12.

[266] Cael. Aurel. morb. chr. I. 5. p 337 Another reading pleases us more, which is as follows:—"Another is called the Lydian mode, which counsels shame to the mind occupied with anger and rage: Another with injected vigor, as in war, which they call the Doric mode, is used in those who are affected by laughter and childish giggling." Perusing this whole chapter of Caelius, no one can doubt that these are descriptions from the books of Asclepiades. Doubtless Caelius reviews various methods of treating madness, mentioning no names of authors But at the end of the chapter (p. 338) he says: "lest these be thought false, people will be named and the names of books designated. Asclepiades teaches that song should be employed second."

[267] Cels. III. 18.

P. 81.   *Certain Things of Much Importance Outlined*
Which Asclepiades Always Followed

1. Already from many things, which thus far we have related, it may be understood how admirably Asclepiades conducted himself in respect to founding and establishing his doctrine. We have seen also how the highest praise is due him which can befall physicians assisting the sick. We have seen that he neglected nothing which ever becomes a physician living near the couches of his patients. This he always considered, that there is nothing certain to tell about diseases and their diagnosis and treatment, since he rightly knew how they vary from weather, air, ages, regions, kind of life, and other things of this sort, and diseases themselves vary, and the strength of drugs. (P. 69, 79) That his merits may shine the more on this account, be it permitted to add the opinions of his sectarians, which certainly savor the true mind of the master. Caelius speaks thus:[268]

"Some physicians among whom are sectarians of Asclepiades, also pay attention to the quality of air which the Greeks call glare, and to time and antecedent cause, and nature and age. They say there is a condition of the air that it should not grow hot, because on account of this it affects many, so that often it produces rheums, or ulcers of the eyes. There are times also, like the end of summer or autumn; for in these, they say, this phrenitic passion is frequent; they say there are antecedent causes, like wine-bibbing or wakefulness and live scorchings: they speak of the nature of the patient as if he were mobile of mind, and wrathful, or trained in the disciplines of letters, or with a weak head and easily feeling a draught, or if often he is affected with illness, and easily troubled with delirium: and they say age, if he is young. All things ought to be foreseen, for significance is confirmed not from one or two, but from many concurrent phenomena: for one certain thing also is common to another. But the combination of many things, concurring into one, makes judgment surpass intelligence."

In the same way, in the treatment of tetanics he notes the distinction which exists between the nature of children, women, and

---

[268] Cael. Aurel. morb. ac. I. 2. p. 12 sq

men.[269] In the treatment of phrenitic disease he has regard to the seasons of the year and adapts the quantity of drink to them.[270]

2. Asclepiades says the duty of a physician is to cure disease safely, quickly, and happily.[271] Admirably then Celsus adds that too much haste and pleasure are almost always dangerous, but that such moderation should be employed that, so far as it can be done, all these results are attained, safety being always the first consideration. That this was also so observed by Asclepiades that always he took first account of safety, there is no one who doubts. Celsus himself recounts that in the first days of a fever he did not care whether the treatment was pleasurable to the patients or not, and that those are in error who maintain that his treatment was pleasant throughout. For in the later days of an illness he even approved of luxury: but at first he played the part of an executioner.[272]

3. It is known that, before the arrival of Greek physicians, the Romans had no medical treatment other than what each provided for himself. Their mind was so blinded by superstitions that, as soon as they were troubled by diseases, they immediately fled, for the help of the gods, to auguries, enchantments, incantations, and other superstitious medications: the medicines which they used were those which the father of the family had regarded with personal and hereditary knowledge: quaint and crude methods of treatment throve, which more increased their sufferings for the sick than served to relieve them. Cato's domestic medicine can be mentioned as an example of all.

When Asclepiades came to Rome, he took pains first to remove that offensive medicine and then to win the favor of men. Hence Pliny says: "many things primitive and crude assisted Asclepiades in the treatment of the ancients, like covering the sick with clothes, provoking sweats in every way; now roasting their bodies at the fire or assiduously seeking the sun in the cloudy city, nay in all Italy."[273] The credulous and superstitious mind of men had reached such a point that it imputed magic virtues even to herbs, some of which

[269] Cael. Aurel. morb. ac. I. 15. p. 51.

[270] Cael. Aurel. morb. ac. III 8. p. 215.

[271] Cels. III. 4.

[272] cf. Dor. Christ. Erxlebiae demonstrating the difference that to cure too quickly and pleasantly often results in less safety of cure. Hal. 1754 and Juncker. in progr.

[273] Plin. H.N. XXVI. 3.

Pliny relates.[274] But although there were already many who themselves perceived that those virtues were vain, that was no impediment to Asclepiades from removing all faith in them. No doubt
Pliny wished to denote the same thing, when he said: "above all
he was assisted by magic vanities, carried so far that they could
abrogate the faith in all herbs."[275]

4. Assuredly it is true, as Celsus says, that he will treat correctly
whom the first origin of cause has not deceived.[276] That it was fixed
and perceived in the mind of Asclepiades, all his doctrine informs
us, and Pliny reports that he refused all treatment to cause.[277] Hence
we can understand what led him to declare that the empiric sect
relied on no secure supports.[278]

5. In salutary precepts he also praises variety of life. Likewise he
denies that the athletic habit is safe.[279]

Many other things, which so far are lacking here, I have reserved,
since they can be better treated in the following chapter.

[274] Plin. l c. cap. 4.
[275] Plin. l.c.
[276] Cels. in praefat.
[277] Plin. H.N. XXVI. 3.
[278] Galen. de subfigurat. emp. cap. 13. p. 346. To. II.
[279] Cael. Aurel. morb. ac. I. 14. p. 44.

Chapter VIII

CONCERNING DIAGNOSIS AND TREATMENT OF DISEASES ACCORDING TO THE DOCTRINE OF ASCLEPIADES

P. 82.   *Division of Diseases*

Asclepiades followed the common classification of diseases when he declared them acute or rapid, and chronic or slow: otherwise febrile or afebrile. To him a disease is called acute which arises suddenly and is quickly resolved.[280]

P. 83.   *Fever*

Asclepiades describes the diagnosis of fever in these words: "it is elevated temperature in all or most parts of the body, with modification of pulse to violent produced on account of obtrusion."[281] But he thinks these signs can also be present although the patient is laboring with no fever, and he says that then only they signify fever if no other cause is present to which they might seem to owe their origin.[282]

These are the diagnostic signs of fever which physicians have kept unchanged from the time when it was permitted to observe febrile patients even to the present day. But concerning their cause and origin they diverge into almost infinite opinions. For everyone is eager to accomodate these things to the principles of the doctrine of which he is the author and patron, and then to establish and confirm his own system. As Erasistratus attributed them to the transition of blood from the veins to the arteries; as Herophilus thinks

[280] This evidently is clear from Cael. Aurel. morb chr III. 8. p. 469 where he relates that Asclepiades declared dropsy either acute or chronic: one with fever, the other without fever. Caelius then continues· "this commonly also he ascribes to other special diseases, not noting that since an acute disease can be called by its own name, not only that which occurs suddenly, but also that which it is shown can be quickly resolved, is so called "

[281] Cael Aurel. morb. ac. II 33. p 151.

[282] Cael. Aurel morb. ac I 14 p 42 Caelius says here. "they (Asclepiades and his sectarians) consider temperature the chief sign of fevers, and transformation of the pulse in violence, unless these manifestations should be from some other cause " Therefore individual signs prove nothing, but all should be present which owe their origin to obtrusion of the corpuscles.

they are the signs of good blood: so to Asclepiades they are signs of obtrusion of the corpuscles, which occurs in the passages or pores.[283] Therefore Asclepiades uses two arguments to prove the occasion whereby fever is produced, of which one is because there are in us certain passages, which are perceived by the mind, differing among themselves in size and shape: the other is because everywhere particles of fluid and of spirit are collected from molecules or corpuscles.[284] Which corpuscles, therefore, if by any impediment they are intercepted in their course through the passages, excite fevers.

But from these things, which we have related above, we have already perceived that Asclepiades imagined a dual kind of corpuscles which are carried through the passages: the corpuscles themselves, and spirit. The corpuscles are either larger or smaller: the smallest constitute spirit. He thinks, therefore, that every variety of fevers is to be regarded in the light of the cause obstructing its

[283] Sext. Emp adv. Logic II. f 220. p. 499: "like the escape of perceptible particles in per ceptible rarefactions."

[284] Sext. Emp (adv. Geom f. 5. p. 311) adds another, third argument, doubtless because there are perpetually being emitted from us vapors, either more or less, according as various things either increase or diminish the amount of them. It is worth while to read his own words, which are as follows —"Thus we say then that Asclepiades employed three hypotheses for explanation of the cause producing fever: first, that there are in us certain perceptible passages differing from one another in size; second that particles of moisture and gas gather together; and third, sometimes more and sometimes less, that these particles come to the orifice and escape For the third argument, Sextus Empiricus wished to understand transpiration, which goes on constantly in the well body, is obvious, and is not, which we doubt, such that Asclepiades could not explain it in the same way as, according to him, all secretions of the body are formed. For as corpuscles, from food digested in the stomach, tend to the urinary bladder and are there eliminated, so the same corpuscles go to the skin, and there are perpetually emitted, constituting transpirable material. Bianchini, disc II P. II, is persuaded of the same thing, and utters the following words· The varying diameter of pores, mediating, accomplishes the separation of different fluids, which serve for nourishment, or growth, or to soften all the parts composing our organs, and continuous universal transpiration is maintained This also is taught by the use of massage and transportation, whereby the passages are made more open, and the body is made thinner. Cael Aurel I 15 p. 52. supra. P. 72. Perhaps also by those vapors is more rightly understood not only transpirable material, but in general all fluids secreted, which, the same as the former, are daily and almost perpetually eliminated from the body From these, therefore, I infer that perhaps Asclepiades thought that those intercepted vapors (suppressed transpiration or other retained secretions) bring it about that obtrusion occurs more easily and that those are the cause of this But that we should believe is counselled both by the entire teaching of Asclepiades and by his method of treatment which he used for fever, as may presently be seen. Hence I know not what it is, disturbed by which Sprengel (Vers einer pragm Gesch. der Arzneik. p. 443) declared: "Fever he explained by increased extenuation of these atoms, whereby it is nevertheless to be suspected that the reference did not properly grasp the meaning of the Bithynian."

way, and that these causes are diverse, according as the cause is located in the corpuscles, or in the spirit. Stagnations of corpuscles
produce severe, violent fevers, like phrenitis, lethargy, and others;
but disturbances of the spirit, and others produce fevers which are
milder, and are easily resolved.[285]

In order that he may explain the varying type of intermittent fevers, he has recourse also to the varying size of corpuscles. He thinks
that the quotidian type is caused by stasis of the larger corpuscles,
which can be more quickly and easily moved: but that the type of
tertian fever is caused by obtrusion of the smaller corpuscles, whose
course can be restored with more difficulty, and which are more slowly
evacuated and eliminated: finally that the type of quartan fever has
such superlatively minute corpuscles as its cause that they can be
propelled only with the greatest and maximal difficulty.[286]

From these details we can also admirably well understand in what
factor, according to the opinion of Asclepiades, is located the distinction between fevers, both those which occur of continuous type
and those of intermittent type. Everything comes down to stagnation of corpuscles, either milder or more severe: if they stagnate
seriously, they excite a continuous or persistent fever: if the stagnation is milder, an intermittent fever occurs: if the fluids or spirit
are only perturbed, the fevers are milder and are soon resolved.[287]

Fevers run through various stages: they increase to maximum
strength, and then decline. They are relieved at daybreak, and accessions are increased at night. The nature of evenings, he says, on
account of the density of the air, inflates the thickened bodies and
produces the beginning of an accession.[288] These are things which

[285] Cael. Aurel morb. ac I. 15. p. 42. "He says that various diseases are produced by di-
versity of places or passages and all by stagnation of corpuscles, but certain ones, phrenitis,
lethargy, pleurisy, and severe fevers, though capable of resolution, by disturbance of fluids
and of spirit."

[286] Cael. Aur. l.c.: "Likewise he declares that the quotidian type is produced by stagnation
of the larger corpuscles: for he says they are quickly evacuated and amalgamated: but the
tertian type is caused by stagnation of the smaller corpuscles. Likewise the quartan type by
stagnation of the smallest. For with difficulty they can be amalgamated and evacuated.

[287] Cael. Aurel. morb. ac. I p. 3. "for as, when speaking of causes, he said, that fever was
severe which was caused by stasis or obtrusion; but that was mild and capable of resolution
which was caused by perturbation of fluid materials and spirit· so also he said that phrenitic disease is severe which is produced by stasis or obtrusion of the corpuscles."

[288] From those things which we have heard before about the origin of sleep, we know that
it comes on, if fluids, especially spirit, or air washing the body all day, become denser: we
know also that they then tend more to the internal parts. (P. 39. P. 52.) Therefore a recent
obtrusion can readily arise, and thence a fresh accession of fever.

warn us of obtrusion of corpuscles; and Caelius speaks as follows in the actual words of Asclepiades.

"But what produces stasis of corpuscles, or obtrusion in what or from what corpuscles, and also how those things which occur in parts disturb the whole body and produce fevers, we have explained in what we have written in the tenth book."[289]

But perhaps from other things which we have learned from the teaching of Asclepiades about fever we can elicit something definite about the origin and nature of certain symptoms. What pertains to the increased heat, which is felt in fevers, we ought to restore to its origin in the healthy state.

But we know that he established its seat in those minutest corpuscles which constitute spirit. (P. 48. not. 126). That he therefore might thence explain febrile heat, he postulated a greater impact and friction of corpuscles. Doubtless when that calorific material not only passes through the slender passages but is mixed with all the body fluids (larger and smaller corpuscles) (46, not. 117), increased warmth cannot fail to arise in fever from greater percussion of corpuscles.[290]

In the contrary way he seems to have explained chill or rigor. Doubtless Galen relates that Asclepiades, when he declared that all fever is excited by certain obstructions of corpuscles in passages, placed the difference of fevers in the varied size of passages, and from this showed that when varied obstruction arises in various larger or smaller passages, rigor is necessarily combined with certain fevers, and not with certain others.[291]

Already it has been often observed by physicians that intermittent fevers, which vex the body through a long space of time, finally dissolve its structure to such an extent that it wastes away and progressively emaciates. Asclepiades had already found this out, too, as Caelius relates in these words. "Asclepiades says that daily con-

---

[289] Asclepiades seems to have made a distinction between fever and feverishness, or the symptoms by which it is constituted. Obtrusion is the cause of feverishness, (which word is a term of description or classification), but feverishness is the cause of fever itself (a term of appellation). Vid. Cael. morb. ac. I. p. 4.

[290] Cael. Aur. morb. ac. I. p 7. "otherwise with fevers, arising because of obtrusion of membranes, small and very mild fevers occur when blows, or impacts, and contacts occur which can cause a minimal rise of temperature for the body."

[291] Galen. de trem. palp. etc. p 369. T. III. "For Asclepiades postulated no intrinsic heat nor any other power, but said that all fever arises from obstruction of masses in the pores, placing the difference in the sizes of the pores, and thus showed that chills are necessarily perceptible in some and not in others.

tinuance, of fever, is not without peril, and that many are led from this into another disease, that is dissolution of the body, or dropsy, supervenes, and whatever can be added by debility of the body."[292]

As for what remains, we ought to say a few words here about the opinion of Asclepiades wherein he believed that fever could be employed for treating some chronic diseases, which cling persistently to the body. Doubtless already many and the most experienced physicians, who have devoted themselves assiduously to the treatment of diseases, have observed that sometimes the more persistent chronic diseases resist all medicines and yield to none of them: but, if by some means a salutary fever arises, they immediately depart from the body within whose inmost recesses they were seen to be lurking. This was well perceived and known to Asclepiades, who, that he might follow nature as a guide, studied in these cases to excite artificially a beneficial fever. So in convulsive disease he employs very powerful enemata and those working more violently, thinking that salutary fever is produced therefrom, whereby the movement and transfer of material from the pathological parts to the intestines is effected.[293]

It is now worth while to discuss briefly the method of treatment which in general he employed for fevers, and which he based not so much on drugs as on regime of living.[294] When he decided that fever originated from obtrusion of corpuscles, nothing more needed to be urged on him, except that he should resolve it: then he always used to consider this, that he should either maintain their strength for his patients, or, if lost, should restore it.[295] But in order that he

[292] Cael. Aurel morb. ac. II 10. p. 98.

[293] Cael. Aurel morb. ac III. 8 p 21E P. 68 From these it can perhaps be inferred that Asclepiades had imagined that fever, or rather the obtrusion from which it derives, if not always, nevertheless often is resolved by nature and eliminated through the intestines For although he denies critical days, nevertheless he believes in critical evacuations (P. 62) Therefore he imitates nature and injects very strong enemata, in order that he may attract stagnant corpuscles to the intestines.

[294] Cels. III 4, and above P. 64–68.

[295] Cels. l.c. "But he professed that he especially uses fever itself for its treatment For he thought that a patient's strength is destroyed by daylight, insomnia, and great thirst, so that he did not even permit the face to be washed in the earliest days For on the later days of an illness, he even approved of luxury, but on the earliest days displayed the mood of an executioner."

But that Asclepiades did not follow these words of Celsus is clear from many passages of Caelius, and that they are to be fully understood only at the first accession of a fever, as he himself rightly notes. Caelius (morb. ac. I. 14. p. 43) mentions that the thirst of patients ought to be endured until the pulse abates.

might act correctly in respect to each method, he noted with all care and diligence the accessions and remissions of a fever; in the former he studies to resolve the fever and to nourish, in the latter to nourish the body. That he may satisfy the first objective of the treatment, he orders to move the bowels, that the obtrusion of corpuscles (P. 68) may be withdrawn and attracted to the intestines. (P. 83. not. 293): he administers drinks in order that he may diminish heat or also dissolve obtrusion itself.[296]

Prominent among those febrile beverages are water, ptisane,[297] spelt,[298] lentil with beet,[299] barley,[300] rice, hyssop,[301] and other things of this sort, which serve this purpose. As soon as the accession has vanished, and the remission begins, he allows solid foods, but those which are moist or nearly liquid, from material as light and delicate as possible.[302] If a new accession supervenes, he uses the described method again, and so continues until complete resolution of the fever. Then he nourishes and strengthens with various foods and with wine. (P. 79)

That which we have especially related is confirmed by what Celsus brings forward concerning the treatment of tertian fever according to the doctrine of Asclepiades.[303] "He himself (Asclepiades), if there is tertian fever, says that the bowels ought to be moved on the third day after the accession; and on the fifth day after the chill, vomiting

[296] Cael Aurel. morb acut. I. 15 p 48 sq morb. ac II 25 p 132. morb. ac II. 29. p.144.

[297] Foef Oecon Hippocr s v Plin. HN XXII f 66.

[298] Pliny seems to oppose (H N XXII. f 61.) speaking thus: "spelt is a Roman preparation, not previously devised; otherwise the Greeks would not rather have written their praises of ptisane I think it was not yet in use in the age of Pompey the Great, and so hardly anything was written about it by the school of Asclepiades."

[299] Both of which Asclepiades called by the Greek name Seuthophace. Cael. Aurel. II 39 p 175. Vid. Sotio Geopon lib. XII. c. 15 Triller Observ. crit lib IV. c. 13. p. 381. Foef Oec Hipp. s v φακή and φακός

[300] Plin H N. XXII f 65. Foef Oec Hipp. s v. κριθή.

[301] Foef. Oec. Hipp. s v.

[302] Vid loc. ex. Caelio cit —Cels. III 4, "The ancients used to offer food to those with bodies as intact as possible; Asclepiades, when the fever has declined but is nevertheless still present." Idem l c. "Asclepiades, when he had carried the patient through everything for three days, used to assign food on the fourth day " Cael Aurel morb ac I. 14 p. 43. proposes the same. Likewise he says "the time of giving is not at complete resolution, but at the decline of accession " In the same way he advises also that food be given on the third and fifth day, but avoided on the second and fourth, since the fever is exacerbated on alternate days Cael. Aurel morb. ac II. 22. p. 132 It is to be noted here that from this method of treatment of Asclepiades subsequently arose the cycles of the Methodici, which hereafter more often there will be opportunity to see in the treatment of individual diseases.

[303] Cels. III. 14.

should be elicited; then after the fever, as was his custom, warm foods and wine should be given.[304] On the sixth day the patient should be kept in bed: for so it would come about that there should not be an accession of fever on the seventh day."

At the close of this discussion it remains that we should mention a rare observation, concerning malignant intermittent fevers, which we owe to Asclepiades. It is known that sometimes intermittent fevers occur accompanied by somnolent seizures and headache, and that these are endemic in certain localities. So Galen, and Baglivius who practiced his profession at Rome, report that double tertians are frequent and malignant in Rome, of whom the latter adds that headache is endemic. And behold, our Asclepiades also already has observed the same thing.

Caelius Aurelianus thus relates his observations: "At Rome," says he, "we have observed that these fevers, (double tertians), are prevalent, with oppression of body and mind, in likeness of a lethargy, which, on the second or third day, are established in a state of accession or onset, with the body immediately warm again, or with diminishing severity, and recall the patients to resumption and moderate recovery. But if once they have ceased with a light attack, once the patient is seized, they will give no recovery, but cease in sweating and rapid respiration and a febrile pulse and become unconscious. And again he writes similarly about these, and not once but frequently, saying that the seizure of the mind occurs in a certain way in the onsets of types, and that this prevails at Rome, giving also the causes whereby these individual phenomena are produced.[305] Caelius also relates that the ancient physicians knew this disease, but confused it with lethargy, which Asclepiades showed to be different and gave it the name of catalepsy.[306]

"Stating his method of treatment, Asclepiades says that if attacks or sensory seizures should occur while the fevers are still delaying and lingering, and if, in the onset, they should produce silence of the voice, other measures, as we said above, having been similarly applied, if three or four hours have been gained before the onset, if the

[304] Cael. Aurel. morb. ac. I. 14. p. 43. teaches us the same. Likewise in Samothrace he approves the enema and emetic about evening of the day before. But, in those who are affected with the periodic types, he prefers the emetic to the enema. But for typical ones he says both enema and emetic should be given, and diluted Samothracian wine to drink."

[305] Cael. Aurel. morb. ac. II. 19. p. 99.

[306] Cael. Aurel. l.c. p. 96.

bowels do not move, we will give a sixth of a drachm of spurge-juice[307] with three or four sixth-drachms of castoreum, with water, anointing the occiput and temples of the head with thapsia[308] or fennel which we call ferula crushed in water, so that it makes a certain sensation and moderate relief over the surface of the body. Likewise he says that more solid foods should be given, unless the precordium should be involved in a swelling: but if this should inter-fere, potable foods should be given."[309] From the same narrative of Caelius, it seems also to be clear that Asclepiades urged that wedges should be placed in the teeth, in order that they may separate, and that the head should be poulticed with cold fomentations, such as ivy-juice.[310]

P. 84.   *Phrenitis*

In the whole first book of his *Acute Diseases*, Caelius Aurelianus inquires into phrenitis, and there indeed copiously, but not clearly and accurately enough so that we can properly establish judgment about them. He brings forward and rejects the opinions of Asclepiades. But we must exercise the greatest diligence in explain-ing both this and other diseases which Caelius describes according to Asclepiades. For in the first place he himself did not understand the teaching of Asclepiades, as can be shown from many things. Then he judges it influenced by his own opinions. Therefore we ought to be extremely careful lest we become involved in the same errors of Caelius. Therefore we have proposed merely to relate those things which, led by the principles of the doctrine of Asclepiades, having been already explored by us, we think really to have been brought forward by him. The opinions of the sectarians of Asclepiades, which are related by Caelius, we clearly omit here, since we do not know which of them are due to the master himself. Now, following Caelius, in the same order, we will explain phrenitis according to the doctrines of Asclepiades. His definition is as follows:—"Phrenitis is a stasis or obtrusion of corpuscles in the membranes of the brain, often without associated sensation, but with alienation and fever." Caelius ad-vises us that Asclepiades himself explained this definition and in his

[307] Spurge or diagridium is the juice of tithymalis or euphorbia, and serves in purging the abdomen. Plin. H N. XXVI. f. 39.
[308] Plin. H N. XIII. f. 43.
[309] Cael. Aurel. morb. ac. II. 12. p. 108.
[310] Cael. Aurel. l.c. p. 109.

first book about acute diseases said that he had put "with fever" in
the definition on this account, since without fever people are sometimes alienated in mind who have drunk poppy or mandragora or
something else or are perturbed by immense anger or excessive fear
or even oppressed by great sorrow or agitated by epileptic disease;
but that he said without associated sensation, lest we should also
think that the pleuritic or the pneumonic are phrenitic, who, in the
intensity of their disease are often agitated by errors of the mind for
seven or eight days.

In his first chapter, Caelius enquires whether these are signs of
future phrenitic disease, which Asclepiades affirms. Doubtless we
know, from what has preceded, that, in differentiating disease, he
took particular account of air, time, antecedent causes, and nature
and age of the patient. (P. 81, 1.) We know also that he divided the
signs of diseases into the essential and the unessential (P. 63). Hence
he could not fail to relate also signs which announce future phrenitis.
This opinion his sectarians have attempted to defend against the
objections of Thessalus, as may be read in many places in Caelius.

In his fifteenth chapter Caelius speaks about the treatment which
Asclepiades employed in phrenitis. We read there that in his first
book of acute diseases he refuted those who postulated that contrary
measures should be employed; that in his second book he taught how
phrenitis might be averted; and that in his third book he taught how
it ought to be treated, when it had occurred. In the same order we
will now relate what Asclepiades said.

Therefore, he disapproves enemata,[311] he disapproves drinking
iris, and vinegar with honey, and he disapproves purging phlegm
with mustard, and shearing. For by shearing, as by a stimulant, a
greater amount of fluids is attracted to the head and the membranes
of the brain become more constricted and tense: the pores and hairs
after shearing become thicker and stronger. Wherefore also men,
sheared after food, are harassed by cough and catarrh or rheum.
Then if, after shearing, we take care to cover the head with woolens,
how much better if it is concealed by a natural covering of hair.

He disapproves also of patients' lying in a dark place. For in a
dark place the sick indulge themselves too much in various fancies,
and are harrassed by imaginings devised in an alienated mind, since

---

[311] Caelius adds no reasons, moved by which Asclepiades forbade the use of enemata. For
he himself orders them to be employed in the cure of phrenitis.

no external phenomena can fall on the senses; but in a bright place they are prevented from being wholly in their own fancies, which are rather weakened by external phenomena, just as the flame of night light and torches, kindled in the daylight, languishes by contrast of something better seen.[312]

He also disapproves venesection. We have already seen above that Asclepiades declared that venesection should be employed only in those diseases which are associated with pain, or which have derived their origin from the larger corpuscles, which alone can be evacuated by venesection. But phrenitis arises from the smallest corpuscles obtruded in the interstices of the membranes of the brain.[313] Therefore venesection does harm in phrenitics.

Doubtless those phlebotomized are affected with mental deficiency and a cold torpor of the body, or sustain a defect of the voice or mental alienation. For there is withdrawn material of the larger corpuscles, but the cause of the disease, or material of the smallest corpuscles, remains, the rest of the blood thickens, and bodily pain arises; the spirit, or fever, is carried to the membrane of the brain, and hence the stasis of corpuscles and the alienation are doubled.[314]

In averting disease and mental alienation, Asclepiades considers in the first place the number of days, the days, of onset and of re-

[312] Cels. III 18. But the ancients generally used to keep such patients in dark places, because they judged that they would be terrified by what was contrary to them, and that darkness contributed something to their peace of mind. But Asclepiades said they ought to be kept in the light, as if the darkness itself were terrifying

[313] Doubtless phrenitis is especially distinguished by alienation of the mind, which, according to Asclepiades, is disease in the senses But these depend on the smallest corpuscles, which cannot be eliminated by venesection (P 48 not 126 and P 69) I gather this from Cael morb. ac. p 6 where he says "Asclepiades thought that the cause of all phrenitis is either substance, or generally alienation· but commonly that the substance of alienation consists in sensations. Finally in books of definitions, defining alienation, he explained it in this way "alienation is disease in the senses." In P 69 above, not , I have studied to prove that Asclepiades, when he said that venesection has a place only in those diseases with which pains are associated, perhaps understood inflammatory pains It occurred to me that by this he meant nothing else than in those diseases in which the patient feels no pains, but is suffering from delusion of the mind, which permits no venesection, since the smallest corpuscles, which are then affected, cannot be expelled by venesection But in those diseases in which the blood is affected with its larger corpuscles, which are emitted by venesection, the patient feels pains on account of common sensation, but the mind itself (with its smallest corpuscles) suffers no harm.

[314] Celsus, l.c offers another argument. "Asclepiades said that there is blood sent to these and so they are destroyed, following this reason, because there would be no insanity, unless the fever were intense, and no blood unless in its remission it were rightly despatched."

mission. On the first day of the first relapse, he urges giving a very little food and, in the expected state of the fever, to give to drink ptisane or barley or spelt, or lentil with beet, or something like these, adding that only the novelty of giving from these is advantageous, and that no account should be taken which of them we ought to offer, but that it should be permitted to the pleasure of the patients which they wish to choose;[315] on the second day, if a little fever continues and persists, he advises to evacuate the obtrusions and to apply rest to the body, and to administer water, but not more than twice a day, up to half a sextarius or two, and to observe this method also at night. On the first day of the second relapse he advises, when the increase of the accession has occurred, to give some one of the soft solids, and on the second day, when the fever is abating, to use soft solid food; but, if the fever persists, to abstain again, and when it is past to imitate a third relapse. Then on the seventh day he uses bread and fishes and wine; for, he says, the disease is often resolved on the third period.[316]

Asclepiades demonstrated a dual treatment of phrenitis; one safe, conservative, or not meticulous, and suitable for many phrenitics; the other dangerous, radical, and violent, which he called venturesome. Employing the former of these methods of treatment, he asks whether the patient has ever been treated by anyone else or not? If this has not yet been done, he uses spices, castoreum or beaver-oil, hog's-fennel or sulphur-wort, rue and vinegar, or a fluid infusion of these, and an enema for the purpose of removing the obtrusion. But, if he has already tried the remedy of some other physician, immediately at the first outset he forbids ointment, plaster, poultice, and spice, changes the patient from darkness to light, employs a sternutatory also, gives wine mixed with honey four times daily in summer, twice daily in winter,[317] a quarter of a sextarius in individual, separate doses; but it is necessary that the honey should be boiled beforehand, lest the bowels should be loose and soft.

Then, when night comes, he should be removed moderately to his abode, and too much or open air should be avoided: then, if there is

---

[315] It should be noted here that each patient is permitted to choose only what he himself drinks of these various beverages.

[316] See what we have noted concerning this method of treatment for three days. P. 85.

[317] Cels. l.c. "There is need of soft food, and especially drinking of honey-water, of which it is enough to give three cups twice in winter and four times in summer.

another accession, or a stupor of the joints, he gives some one of the potable prescriptions: but if the signs of fever should remain without remission, immediately at evening he anoints the entire body with oil, but the head and neck with oil of roses, and gives liquid food; then, if he employs a sitting transportation, the motion will be sufficient for bestowing sleep, for it soon makes the sick soft and gentle.[318] Finally some of the phrenitics become unconscious because of motion when the body is emaciated. Wherefore it is more fitting to employ transportation at night and after food.[319] (P. 72)

The hazardous, radical, venturesome treatment he so designed that almost everything which he employed differed not at all from his previous method of treatment, except wine, which, if their disease requires it at all, they drink instead of honey in the evening: but if not, immediately at the outset he gives both diluted, that is pure and extended, wine, which he called salted. (P. 79)

Doubtless he thought that, for the small benefits which resulted from beverages and honey, greater would come from wine. For from that, running through the whole body and burning into sensation, as more heat arises from a cautery, and stimulation of the pulse, the dissolving perspiration is abated.[320]

P. 85.   *Lethargy*

Asclepiades himself demonstrated no definition of this disease; but Alexander of Laodicea, his pupil, according to himself says that lethargy is an acute, rapid, or sudden disease, with fever, and pressure, and difficulty of coördinating the senses.[321] He says that the

---

[318] Celsus l.c. reports that Asclepiades advised massage to this end. "If nevertheless they are wakeful, some get to sleep by giving water for a drink in which poppy or hyssop have been boiled. Many use cooked pods of poppy, in which water they bathe the face and head with a sponge. Asclepiades says this is superfluous, since they often pass into lethargy. But he teaches that on the first day the patient should refrain from food, drink, and sleep; in the evening he should be given water for a beverage; then gentle massage should be given, so that not even the hand which rubs should be forcibly applied: then on the following day, when all the same things have been done, in the evening he should be given a drink of water and again massage should be applied. For by this we shall secure the onset of sleep. Sometimes it happens that, by his admission, too much massage also brings on the danger of lethargy.

[319] Cels. l. c.: transportation after food and at night also contributes something to sleep.

[320] Doubtless under this hazardous treatment is to be understood that malignant phrenitis in which the pulses are found more feeble, and there is extreme prostration of strength with dissolution of the humors.

[321] Cael. Aurel. morb. ac. II. 1. p. 72 sq.

pulse and respiration are fuller and gentler in lethargics than in phrenitics: likewise the pulse has a size and stronger beat, as of those sleeping soundly. In the first book of the acute diseases he said that the phrenitics differ from the lethargics in this, that the former suffer from alienation and delusion with mania, but the latter with stupor and depression. Some sectarians of Asclepiades also describe varieties of lethargics; for they say one has it spontaneously; another from a previous illness, like phrenitis: and when spontaneous, it is never severe: one is recent, another is old and chronic, which they said can be conjectured from the number of days: one happens to a body affected with acidity and plethora: another to one empty and macerated with disease.[322]

Asclepiades, writing in his first book about acute diseases, says that many things should be employed for lethargics which were ordered for phrenitics. He studies also continually to arouse the stuporous with sternutatories, and spices, and castoreum, with rue and vinegar, with cow-parsnip,[323] with flea-bane,[324] and willow,[325] herbs. He also recommends bayberries and everything that can thin and move vigorously the membranes of the brain. He orders also to apply those things which he gave to epileptics or to those with suffocation of the womb to smell, wool, or hair, or stag's horn, or galbanum placed on coals, and everything which can make the head heavy or is unpleasant to smell.[326] Best of all and most effective he thinks is powder of mustard, mixed with vinegar; and with this the head should be poulticed and it should be given by hand to stimulate the patient.[327] He gives a drink two or three times a day; and when night comes on he offers wine to the phrenitics, even more boldly.[328] For, he says, it is possible to add fury to phrenitics with wine, but never

[322] Cael. Aurel. l.c cap. 5. p. 80. sq.

[323] Plin H.N. XXIV. I. 16. Cow-parsnip is poured on the heads of phrenitics and lethargics.

[324] Plin. H.N. XXI. f 32.

[325] Plin. H.N. XXIV f. 38. Cooked willow-seed in oil is instilled on the head in lethargy and in phrenitis.

[326] Cels. III 20 "Some then strive to stimulate these patients by giving those things whereby sneezing is provoked, and those which move by their foul smell, such as crude pitch, freshly shorn wool, pepper, hellebore, castoreum or beaver-oil, vinegar, garlic, onion; they even burn galbanum, or hair, or hartshorn. If it's not this, something else. For when these are burned they release a foul stench " Plin. H N. XX f 20 mentions that the school of Asclepiades thought that lethargics are aroused by an onion

[327] Cels. l.c · "a frontal application of mustard to the head is particularly effective for exciting a man when applied to the nostrils, and for warding off disease itself."

[328] Cels. l.c. "Wine also, with timely administration of food, helps not a little."

to lethargics: for all the senses can be conscious, and the vigor of the mind overcome.

P. 86. *Pleurisy*

Asclepiades, in his book of definitions, says that "pleurisy is a brief and rapid flow[329] of rheum, over the interior parts of the side, with fever and swelling.[330] In this he agrees with Diocles and Erasistratus, because the pleura, which they call the underlying membrane, lining the flanks and interior, is the place affected.[331]

From the second volume of his *Acute Diseases*, it is clear that Asclepiades did venesection on pleuritics; but nevertheless he always considered this, whether or not the region where the patients resided would permit venesection. For he testifies that among the Athenians and Romans, pleuritics did badly and were upset after venesection; but that in Parium and the Hellespont, they recovered and were relieved (P 69). Also he forbids injecting enemata: but if they were really required for the sake of emptying the bowels, he advises employing them once or twice. He also forbids thirst, or drinking before food. More and most he gives honey as a beverage, sometimes also both rue and hyssop with the honey. He says that the root of the herb which the Greeks call mullein is harmful.[332] Wherefore he denies altogether that it should be given, or only at the peak, when pain compels. He thinks food should be given, avoiding the second day, if the fever is exacerbated on alternate days: and on the fourth day, if it is more severe: but on the fifth and on the third day he gives barley: and, as is often sufficient, he approves of giving it once daily. But if the patients have failed more, he permits that they should be fed also after the accession of the fifth day: but when the illness declines, he gives wine and various foods.[333]

P. 87. *Pneumonia*

The sectarians of Asclepiades say that pneumonia is a brief suppuration with swelling and fever: suppuration they say on account

---

[329] According to Asclepiades, rheumatism, or a flow of rheum, is when, in the diseases, fluids are emitted by the various excretory passages. Hence pleurisy is a flow of fluid, increased on account of sputum In the same way cholera is a flow of fluid, since fluids are eliminated by vomiting and dejection. See Cael. Aurel morb. ac. III. 19 p. 254.

[330] Cael. Aurel. morb. ac. II. 13. p. 111.

[331] Cael. Aurel. l.c. cap. XVI. p. 115.

[332] Plin. H.N. XXV f. 73. and 74.

[333] Cael. Aurel. morb. ac. l.c. cap. XXII. p. 131. sq.

of the discharge of fluids:[334] brief, that it may be shown different from the phthisic disease, which is also itself the elimination by cough of suppuration and of escaping fluid. They say pneumonia for distinction from other diseases; brief, (as we said above) for satisfaction of eyes or ears resting upon it: they have added also with swelling. If suppuration, that is, escape for a short time from the lung, let that be pneumonia at those parts without fever.[335]

Asclepiades thinks that in pneumonia those parts of the lungs are affected which are attached to the trachea, and which they call the bronchi.[336] Asclepiades thinks that most pneumonics, with a few exceptions, are affected by no pain.[337] Hence also he refuses venesection; for if it were employed from the outset, the blood would come out thin and watery. (P. 69) He prohibits also poultices and steaming; he disapproves enemata and all purgative medicines.—He gives hyssop with honey-water, or goat's thyme. When the disease is abating, he says, poultices should be applied, and he thinks that the patients should be nourished on the rougher days with foods.[338]

P. 88.   *Cardiac Disease*

The sectarians of Asclepiades say that this is an enlargement of the heart, produced by accumulation or obtrusion of corpuscles.[339] There is difference of opinion whether cardiacs are febrile or not, which some affirm and others deny. Asclepiades in his books, which he made contradictory to Erasistratus, maintains that most cardiacs are febrile. For, according to him, fever is maximal heat in all or most parts of the body, with change of pulse in strength caused on account of the obtrusion. (P. 83) But in cardiacs the pulse is not larger, but more shallow: not strong, but weaker: and the heat is not maximal, but less in other parts of the body, and altogether least in the middle.—But nevertheless, in the second book of his "acute diseases", he says that this disease not always, but frequently, occurs with fever.[340]

Erasistratus and Asclepiades have said that the heart is severely affected in cardiacs, and they say that they have benefited by the

[334] See P. 86, not. s.
[335] Cael. Aurel. morb. ac. II. 26. p. 137.
[336] Cael. Aurel. l.c. cap. 28. p. 139.
[337] Cels. IV. 7. This kind of disease has more danger than pain.
[338] Cael. Aurel. l.c. morb. ac. cap. 29. p. 143 sq.
[339] Cael. Aurel. morb. ac. II. 51. p. 146.
[340] Cael. Aurel. l.c. cap. 33. p. 150.

mere name of the disease, since indeed it is called cardiac disease because it arises from the heart. For the Greeks call what pertains to the heart cardiac. There they confirm their opinion by this, because there seems to be a leap in it, and in the left side, at the nipple, a heaviness of the chest. Then they are assisted by the magnitude of the disease itself, which could not be, unless some principal part of the body were affected. But the heart is an outstanding and beneficent portion of the body, supplying blood and spirit to all the members. (P. 48. not. 126)[341].

Asclepiades says that cardiacs, and those who suffer from weakness of the stomach, differ in this, that in cardiacs the pulse is very small and weak, but the leap of the heart greater and violent with heaviness in the chest and choking respiration. But in those who are failing with stomach trouble, the pulse is strong in the other arteries, but the leap of the heart is weak, and other symptoms are different in each disease.[342]

In the second book of his *Acute Diseases*, he suspects that there may be some hyperacidity in the body: hence he employs very effective enemata, on account of the recurrence which ought to take place (P. 68). After the injection he employs a poultice of the left mamillary region, of constrictive virtue: but, for the sake of excluding frigid torpor, he approves of warming it with inunctions of old oil, and rubbing with warm hands and cloths the surrounding regions, from which aforesaid regions the warming and inunctions we have declared should be excluded. But constrictive poultices should be applied not only to the left mamillary region but to the whole chest and precordium. He also orders wine to be given at night, by day, and continuously: but this is wine, with which brine has been mixed and which he called salted. "For quickly," he said, "it runs, and flows, and reaches all members of the body." (P. 47). As food he gives beet with lentil, which he called seutlophace; or lentil with barley, or rice, or spelt, or something from the maritime foods; and he says it is proper for us to give whatever else is most pleasing to the patient's taste.[343]

[341] Cael. Aurel. l.c. cap. 34. p. 154.
[342] Cael. Aurel. l.c. cap. 35. p. 156.
[343] But note here what Celsus (III, 6) says on this subject: "but various foods should finally be set before the patient (as Asclepiades teaches) when he is urged by his taste, and his strength is not sufficiently maintained, that by tasting a little of individual foods he may avoid hunger. But if neither strength nor desire is lacking, the patient should not be tempted by any variety, lest he should consume more than he can digest." See P. 84.

But Asclepiades approves that wine should be given after food, lest it should pass through the intestines too quickly (P. 79). He also orders pure wine to be given undiluted. For in this way, he says, burned passages, as if slightly conductile, retain the moisture. Nothing is known whether he gave wine cold or warm. But since, in the books which he wrote about plague, he accused the sectarians of Cleophantus because they gave it cold, it is very likely that he himself advised it warm.—Finally at the end of this description of treatment, Caelius adds:—"This is that famous Asclepiades cooling and warming, evacuating and replenishing, and always using opposite things in these diseases.[344]

P. 89.   *Quinsy*

Defining this disease, in his second book explanatory of the aphorisms of Hippocrates, Asclepiades says, "quinsy is a flow of fluid or moisture from the fauces or of a discharge from them falling by suppuration from the head."[345]

In his second book of "*acute diseases*" Asclepiades withdraws blood in quinsy, and purges the abdomen, and applies poultices, and mouth-washes, and gargles, and in addition attenuating and relaxing inunctions, of hyssop, of marjoram, of thyme, clover, wormwood, cooked fig, saltpetre, larkspur, felwort, cucumber, bull's bile, and cedar oil; and he also advises the use of the cupping-glass with scarification. He denies that any blood can be elicited, either when the disease is with fever, or because the major cause is the swollen parts, which, by contrary impulse, overcomes the warmth of the cupping-glass, so that it cannot accomplish a removal. Then he approves that venesection should be done either from the frontal vein, or at the angles of the eyes, or from the veins under the tongue,

---

[344] Cael. Aurel morb ac l c cap 39 p 174 sq. "It seems very likely to me that Celsus (III, 19) is plainly describing the treatment of cardiac disease according to the concept of Asclepiades. He says that this disease is nothing else than excessive weakness of the body because, with the stomach languishing, it is consumed with immoderate perspiration, the pulse is sluggish and weak Moreover the perspiration is excessive both in manner and in time, and breaks out from the thorax and neck and even the head, only the feet and legs being drier and cooler. But when the disease is of this kind, the first treatment is to place on the precordium constrictive poultices; the second is to prevent perspiration. The third aid is to support the weakened patient with wine and food. In this way no one will regret contributing details of the treatment.

[345] Cael. Aurel. morb. ac. III. 1. p. 181.

or from the arm (P. 69). But if the disease were greater, the fauces should be scarified, that is the tonsils, and the parts established above the uvula; for an equal, or equivalent, incision, which he called homoeotomous, is of the greatest aid. Then he approves of the division of the trachea approved by the ancients, to be done on account of the respiration, which they call laryngotomy or tracheotomy.[346]

P. 90.   *Spasm*

This discussion is about the distinction which exists between spasm and tremor; and, according to Asclepiades, extension and contraction of the parts is slow and persistent: but spasm is of very brief duration, and tremor is very rapid.[347]

In his second book of *"acute diseases"* Asclepiades teaches that, at the onset of pain, tetanics should be poulticed night and day with warm water, then wrapped in bags made of millet, or rosemary, or salt. He thinks also that dry steamings cure more effectively than poultices.—The simple poultice is appropriate, he says, which they call the "raw poultice" of corn meal,[348] for children, women, and men whose bodies are soft and tender (P. 81).—He employs also very strong enemata, thinking that carried by these, a transfer of material may be made from the affected parts of the intestines. (P. 68, P. 83). He also approves of very warm vapors, ordering the affected parts to be steamed with a bag full of salt and hot water. Then the salts are burned with two alternate cauteries, so that a certain amount of vapor, invading from them, may penetrate more deeply. Kindling and lighting a large fire, and placing the patient over it, he rubs all the vertebrae of the spine constantly day and night with oil (P. 71). He says also that he approves the cupping-glass as more useful for this disease, unless fevers prevent the removal of material by this means: but in the veins there would be a greater abundance of blood. For then venesection will be applicable at the peak of severity. For removal of corpuscles, he says, could be done with difficulty at the time of remission. (P. 69). When the disease abates, he feeds the patients with liquids and soft solids.[349]

---

[346] Cael. Aurel. l.c c. 4. p. 193. Cels. IV. 4. Galen. introd. p. 381. T. IV.
[347] Cael. Aurel morb. ac III. 7. p 208.
[348] See Lex. Coelian S.V.
[349] Cae. Aur. l.c. cap. 8. p. 214 sq.

P. 91. *Ileus*

In his third book of *"acute diseases"* Asclepiades defined this disease as follows: "The anguish is an extensive and prolonged torsion of the intestines".[350]

In the third book of his *"acute diseases"* he orders some welcome and effective remedies to be applied, among which is also prohibition of vapor-baths of warm water, as too easily chilling: but he says that the affected parts should be rubbed with oil for a considerable time and thoroughly, as much as the regions themselves can tolerate: (P. 71) but, says he, baths should be shunned even at the time of recession.[351]

P. 92. *Cholera*

In his book about terms Asclepiades gives this definition of the disease: "Cholera is a flow of fluid, rapid and brief, from the abdomen and intestines, from the accumulation or obtrusion of corpuscles, and, as often happens, taking its origin from indigestion.[352]

He produces vomiting from the beverages devoured in greedy draught, and on the same day bathes the patients and administers wine with their drink: he approves most of the old cures, only forbidding that they should be bathed that day, unless their strength should have been restored.[353]

P. 93. *Colitis and Dysentery*

According to Asclepiades diarrhea is rheumatism, or a flow of short duration (P. 86.) from the terminal portions of the colon and sigmoid, or rectum,[354] as we call them, which is, he says, from the accumulation and gathering of corpuscles, with distention.[355] From Celsus[356] we know that Asclepiades advised cold drinks. (P. 77).

P. 94. *Epilepsy*

Among the causes of epilepsy Asclepiades numbers blows on the head, laceration of the membranes which cover the brain, or excessive fear.[357]

[350] Cael. Aurel. III. 17. p. 235.
[351] Cael. Aurel. l.c. p. 245. Cels.
[352] Cael. Aurel. morb. ac. III. 19. p. 235.
[353] Cael. Aurel. l.c. p. 263. Cels IV. 11.
[354] Rectum. See Du Cange Glossar. med. et. infin. latin. s.v. Lexic. Coelina. s.v.
[355] Cael. Aurel. morb. ac. III. 22. p. 265.
[356] Cels. IV. 19.
[357] Cael. Aurel. morb. chr. I 4. p. 291.

In the first book of his *"acute diseases"* he orders that only those who are affected by seizure of the body should have venesection done.—And he orders that an enema should be injected into them, or a collyrium which they call date, with foul odors employed, (P. 85) and fumigations and vinegar which is injected in the nostrils, and the wrapping completed in muslin. He prohibits meat foods, and wine, but orders game.[358]

P. 95.   *Mania*

We know, from those things which (P. 80) we have related, that Asclepiades used music in the treatment of this great disease. Then Caelius reports that Titus, led by his authority, advised compelling maniacs with scourges; but Themison, after venesection, cured them with constrictive poultices, not neglecting baths, more wine, and intercourse: which are more attributable to Asclepiades than to Themison, for his sect had not liberated itself when he was seen to have given such orders as these.[359]

P. 96.   *Paralysis*

Asclepiades wrote nothing about paralysis; but he maintained against Erasistratus that those who are not affected by severe pain in that disease would not have venesection done. But he approves that those who, deprived of their senses, are afflicted with worse compression, should first abstain and then begin again.[360]—He employs also purgative medicines which the Greeks have called cathartics.—But for those in whom there is flaccid paralysis, he says caustic medicines are appropriate and a little poulticing.—Moreover he advises perambulation in a sandy area, with what they call a moat and a bridge of timbers (P. 74), and drinking wine at long intervals.[361]

P. 97.   *Catarrh*

The ancient physicians, among whom are Erasistratus, Themison, and Asclepiades, in the third book of acute diseases and in chronic diseases, have ordered that unmixed wine should be given. For Asclepiades says that the quantity of wine of the customary dilu-

---

[358] Cael. Aurel. l.c. p. 521 sq. Cels. III. 23.
[359] Cael. Aurel. morb. chr. I. 5. p. 339.
[360] He recommends venesection, others evacuation, as Amman advises in the margin ad. h.l.
[361] Cael. Aurel. morb. chr. II. 1. p. 364. Cels. III. 27.

tion should be doubled or tripled, so that he ordered one cup of wine to be mixed with one of water, whereby the quantity of wine and of water are equal. But he does this in the chronic disease. For treating the recent and acute disease, in the book which he wrote to Geminius, he states that wine, though beneficial, should be prohibited. (P. 79)[362]

P. 98.   *Haemorrhage*

Asclepiades postulated two reasons for which blood escapes from the body contrary to nature,—putrefaction of infection, and trauma: he denies anastomosis.[363]

Of those with hemoptysis, he thinks the moist and nummular are difficult of cure on account of their labored respiration: for the same reason also children and the middle-aged; for he says the spirit moves more rapidly, and is delayed in forming the sputa by the resistance of the flesh.[364] Some order their patients to lie flat, or on the unaffected parts: others have persuaded themselves the contrary. So Asclepiades, so far as pertains to position of lying, thinks that the sick should be placed on their affected parts: doubtless when he writes that cures are by necessity, on learning the cause, he orders them thus to be placed when they are determined to be flowing with blood.—In the book, in which he wrote about enemata, he approves of venesection, and says that the veins should be evacuated, where they diverge widely and more quickly yield and unite before they divide,[365] for diminishing the flow of blood, or the breathing, from which the disease becomes worse.[366]

Erasistratus approves ligation at the joints, especially at the groins and the axillae. But Asclepiades, writing preparatory books against him, disapproves ligation, and demonstrates to Erasistratus that it is inconsistent, since veins cannot anastomose below the midriff, which the Greeks call the diaphragm, which above the diaphragm they are seen to do.[367]

---

[362] Cael. Aurel. morb. chr II. 8. p. 385. sq Cels. IV. 2.

[363] Cael. Aurel. morb. chr. II. 10 p. 390

[364] Cael. Aurel. morb. chr 1 c cap. 12. p. 396

[365] Doubtless Asclepiades wished to denote the ample incisions which are made into veins, in order that the blood may be emitted more quickly, and so the flow of blood and difficulty of respiration be more easily mitigated

[366] Cael. Aurel. morb chr. 1 c. cap. 13. p. 415.

[367] Cels. IV 4 "Of these, Erasistratus used to ligate the crural and the femoral and the

Erasistratus approves constrictive poultices; which Asclepiades disapproves, since they repress material and push it deeper.—He forbids transportation in those with hemoptysis. (P. 72.)[368]

P. 99.   *Gastric Disease*

Concerning this disease Asclepiades related nothing else than that a servant of Praxagoras took three two-pound loaves of bread every day, and after eating these was not otherwise affected by disease than if he had had nothing.[369]

P. 100.   *Dropsy*

Asclepiades said that one form is acute, which is suddenly established, and another chronic, which troubles with a slow disease; and another with fever, and another without fever.[370]

He attaches great importance to paracentesis, which he describes diligently. For he thinks that a fistula ought to be left after it is performed.—He testifies that sudden effusion and accumulation is fraught with danger. Doubtless the passages, which the Greeks call pores, when filled with fluid touch one another with a smooth contact, and on this account the patients notice it when they touch; but when removal of the fluids has been made, they touch with a rough contact, and falling together are contracted: and in the same way, the spirit, rushing violently into the flesh, creates pain and distention and cramps of the intestines. After complete removal of the fluid, he employs abstinence.[371]

In the book which he wrote about dropsy, when a little fluid has collected or more, but the feet and legs are not yet affected, he thinks the rule of athletes should be applied, and he dispels the fluids from the retained spirit with more perambulation and running and massage; (P. 71) then he urges upon them bread diligently kneaded, and more exercise, with fishes hard by nature. But if the dropsy has occupied the dependent parts, he forbids most motion and drugs which discharge the fluids from the intestines and urinary passages. He

---

brachial in several places Asclepiades was not so keen on this, but even opposed it." This whole passage of Celsus should be perused, that the argument of Asclepiades may be better understood.

[368] Cael Aurel. morb. chron ., l. c. p. 416, 417.
[369] Cael. Aurel. morb. chr. III. 2. p. 436.
[370] Cael. Aurel morb. chr. III. 8. p. 469.
[371] Cael. Aurel. morb. chr. l.c. p. 478 and 480.

employs paracentesis, but orders it stopped when the liquids flow. But in leucophlegmasia he employs massage and cooling poultices of cydonian apple, and myrrh, and vitis anulis, which they call helix, and Carthaginian apple, and pulse, and old barley, and alum or rue, and onion, and honey, and marjoram, and thyme, and salt-petre, and figs; and he approves of applying an illision of bladders.

He approves also a puncture four fingers from the talus in distance, to be made above, on the medial aspect, as serves in venesection, so that by the fluid poured out through this puncture the body may be relieved: if not, he employs scarification higher up, a stronger and efficacious aid, nor does he fear wounds, which of necessity in this sort of diseases create difficulties in treatment.[372]

But concerning this scarification Aetius speaks with many and different words; and assuredly no one will regret reading that whole passage repeated here in type, since it is plainly described according to the purpose of Asclepiades[373]:

"On the authority of Asclepiades, surgery excels as a more effec-tive aid than all the aforesaid in this kind of dropsy. But it is neces-sary to inflict the incisions around the medial malleolus in a region extending four fingers distance above the talus, to such a depth as anyone would use in venesection. For when a little blood has been evacuated in the first place, for the rest of the time, indefinitely, the evacuation of an equal amount proceeds without any inflammation, so that neither can the incision be closed until all the fluid has first been evacuated, and the patient left slender: and this happens quickly, if no infection seizes the incision; but it itself is permanent for a certain appropriate time, in which everything foreign is elim-inated by itself and there is no need of an extrinsic drug. Moreover no danger need be feared here, as in the tapping of dropsy ascites, for it is not evacuated collectively, like that.

But, in truth, when considerable elimination has been made, if anyone wishes to check it, nothing prevents him from packing lint into such incisions and constricting them with ties; and when again we wish anything to come out, we loosen the ties and remove the lint, and by standing up and moving the patient, provoke excretion."

[372] Cael. Aurel. l.c. p. 489. Cels. III. 21. This passage of Celsus is worth reading entire. For I am convinced that no one will doubt that Celsus outlines everything according to our ideas.

[373] Aetii Tetrab. III. Serm. II. cap. 30 p. 544. ed. Steph. med. art. princ. Conf. Cael. Aurel. morb. ac. I. 14. p. 43.

In a patient, who from a quartan fever had passed into dropsy, Asclepiades relates that he used a two-day abstinence and massage, and on the third day, being already free from both fever and fluid, gave food and wine.[374]

We have also ascertained from Caelius that Asclepiades mentioned that Herodicus, the author of gymnastic medicine, treated dropsy with purgations, vomiting, and vapor baths.[375]

According to our author, Caelius states in these words what dropsy is: "dropsy," he says, "is produced by perforation of the flesh in the form of small passages, which can make unequal the wonted nutriments of the body."[376] The knowledge of this definition doubtless ought to be repeated from the first elements which it has produced concerning the structure of the living body. Since he determined that our body is composed of passages and of corpuscles flowing in them, it is very likely that he is convinced that those parts which constitute flesh in a dropsical condition are characterized and distinguished by many smaller passages. It is necessary that nutriments, therefore, which can enter these small passages, should be dissolved into the smallest particles, of which water is composed.

P. 101.   *Arthritis*

Caelius merely states that Asclepiades, in his book against Erasistratus, wrote something about arthritis.[377] Nothing further is known.[378]

P. 103.   *Hunger and Looseness*

Asclepiades thinks that hunger is caused by largeness of the passages of the stomach and abdomen; but that loss of weight and fluxion of the body and uncontrollable looseness are caused by smallness of the passages.[379]

P. 103.   *Baldness*[380]

Plutarch records that about the time of Asclepiades elephantiasis was first observed in Italy.[381] Since baldness is also associated with

[374] Cel. l.c.
[375] Cael. Aur. morb. chr. l.c. p. 485.
[376] Cael. Aur. morb. ac. I. 14. p. 42.
[377] Cael. Aurel. morb. chr. v. 2. p. 566.
[378] Cf. Galen. VIII. p. 90.
[379] Cael. Aurel. morb. ac. I. p. 42.
[380] vid. Bernard. ad Theoph. Nonn. cap. 8. p. 44. T. I.
[381] Plutarch. symposiac. lib. VIII. p. p. 731. Cf. Hensler's Geschichte des Aussatz, p. 202.

those diseases in which elephantiasis occurs, we can easily understand why Asclepiades speaks in many places of this, of which descriptions are read in Galen, who describes this kind of disease and
his treatment of it to our mind in such eloquent words that we can
hardly include everything in our description, up to the minutest
details. Therefore it seems sufficient to report Galen's own description, which assuredly is of much importance, since it informs us
about the first traces of elephantiasis.[382]

"I now make mention not of the more recent Asclepiades
Pharmacion, who wrote memorable compositions of drugs in many
books, but of the older, namely the Bithynian. This Asclepiades,
then, boasted that he had found a way of treatment by which he
says he has cured many having baldness difficult to be cured. But
he says that the whole regime of living is more important than the
drugs themselves. Concerning this regime, he writes as follows:

"It is necessary, therefore, to abstain completely from all wines,
for the following reasons: it is obvious that he referred to them the
antecedent causes, which if anyone wishes to learn, he requires reading of the book itself. Then he adds that the patient must abstain
also on account of too much repletion. Moreover he forbids also the
eating of meats and cheese and milk and legumes, and in short of
all foods which have strength of a slight recognized amount, whereby
they are both highly nutritious and weight-gaining." But he also
orders to avoid much exercise, just as also continuous baths and
much perspiration.

But concerning drugs he writes next in turn as follows: "first there
is the following ointment: two parts of foam of saltpetre and one
part of salammoniac, rubbed and diluted with very tart vinegar
until it has the thickness of scrapings, lightly applied to the previously scratched bald area, whereby the region is moderately thickened and rendered bloody, then rub until the scalp absorbs it and
the drug sinks down deep, and so let it rest until we get through to
twilight.

Afterwards repeat again at evening, and similarly on the second
and third day, when we find a great transformation. For now the
feeding ceases, and while the hairs are sprouting they are not pulled.
Then on the following day we apply a poultice rubbed in vinegar, in

---

[382] Galen. de medic. compos. fac. loc. lib. I. To. II.

order that blebs may arise, and the skin on the surface become ulcerated. But the blebs are where we divided it, and after two days we find it watery from the ulcers, and then we use the same ointment again, sparing the ulcerated places and passing over them.

But when we find them healed and scrape over them, we leave them quiet until evening; then repeat the same, and continue doing this with much rubbing until the seventh or eighth day.

Then at length we shall see from the limits of the baldness, no longer thin and downy hairs as before, but more robust and sturdy, and afterwards gradually growing out from the denuded parts, and in turn slender and weak hairs lacking; and something similar also happens which we shall see in the ulcerated area. For in the ulcers the scar makes its beginning from the edge and terminates in the centre and unites with others.

So they first get well in the hairy parts near the baldness, and the thick hairs return: but when they are finally situated in the middle of all, then they produce hairs. And if the treatment proceeds in this way, then we shall have no need of any further medicines, but use only this one always for a long time: and the disease yields benignly, unless an altogether large bareness exists.

But in the intervening time we expose the scalp assiduously to open heaven. For sometimes, when the skin is wounded by some sharp point, we elicit blood moderately through the incisions themselves."

These things Asclepiades said first in these words, then spoke about shaving, which others opposed. For not continuously but at intervals, he bids to shave the affected part, that now moderately stiff hairs may arise in it: but when they still come out thin, he does not think it worth while.

But after he has made mention of shaving, then he writes these words: "but if truly the origin of the hairs is delayed, then we have recourse to the following compositions: they are as follows:

Skunk-cabbage-head or its bark burned and rubbed or smothered in smeared honey. Otherwise burn together a sea-horse and a little saltpetre, mixed and smeared with goose-fat in place of saltpetre.

Otherwise, smear some Thapsia softened in water. Otherwise smear some mouse-dung rubbed in vinegar. Otherwise burn some leaves of Calamus Cyprius in a jar, then take plenty of pine resin ashes and place on the previously scarified bald area and bandage.

Or take the bark or crown of reed prepared in the same way, or mix more bread with ashes of saltpetre, and use pitch by exception. This is not weak but more efficacious.''

But after this, Asclepiades also remembers flies, ordering as many of their heads as possible, soon after being captured, to be rubbed on the bare parts of the bald area; and this especially, when the bald area is ulcerated. For, he says that then the blood of the flies carries irritations by the medicines, which are doubtless composed of salt-petre and leeks, since the flies do not bite these themselves only, but also excite blebs in them.

P. 104.   *Hydrophobia*

From the same passage of Plutarch[383] we learn also that it was the opinion of some that that horrible kind of disease distinguished by the name of hydrophobia first began to infest man around the age of Asclepiades. But it is placed beyond all doubt that this disease was known to the more ancient physicians.[384]

Asclepiades indeed wrote nothing about hydrophobia, and his scribes relate nothing; but some of his sectarians doubtless outlined their master's opinions, which Caelius has left us. It is for us to de-scribe them here briefly.

Some of his sectarians think that the affected place is the mem-brane of the brain. If, according to Asclepiades, every disease which disturbs the mind is located in membranes of the brain, they could not hence ascribe hydrophobia to the same membranes: others con-tend that the diaphragm is affected, since the pain is located in it. Artorius* surmises from the hiccough, from the vomiting of bile, and from the insatiable dislike of drinking that the oesophagus is part of the cause; but that the cerebral membranes are affected only in sympathy: others are convinced that the abdomen also is affected with the stomach.[385]

Artorius mentions that certain physicians placed hydrophobics in a vessel full of cold water, or in a well, enclosed in sacs, so that of

[383] Plutarch. symp. VIII, 9.
[384] Cf. Perill. Gruneri. morbor. antiq. sec. III. P. III. p. 234. et Anon. tract de hydroph. ex edit. Bernard.
[385] Cael. Aurel. morb. acut. lib. III. 14. p. 224.
* Friend and personal physician of Augustus in his campaign against Brutus and Cassius in 42 B.C. He was drowned at sea after the Battle of Actium, 31 B.C.

necessity they might be compelled to drink. But he disapproves this method, which afflicts the sick with violence and kills them.[386]

P. 105.   *The Origin of Inflammation*

Inflammation is known from the symptoms which constitute it— from redness, heat, pain, and swelling. All the leaders of sects agree in this, that these symptoms derive from too great a quantity of blood stagnating in some part of the body; and every authority seeks to explain them according to his established system. Hence Asclepiades says that inflammation is produced, if the smallest corpuscles stagnate in the smallest passages.[387]

P. 106.   *A Fragment of Great Importance Which is Left to us from the Writings of Asclepiades.*[388] *Spontaneous Dislocation after Long Disease; By Asclepiades the Bithynian*

In his books on the joints, Hippocrates gives testimony that in those afflicted with long disease, joints may become spontaneously dislocated without obvious cause; and I also have encountered two cases. One was a man at Parium, who had been neither struck nor injured, but his leg at first became painful, and, when he had lain in bed more than three months, it became abducted and dislocated the head of the femur outward, though suffering this without too great severity of pain that I know.

The other case I encountered was a young tragic poet: for in him also, without manifest cause, the femur dislocated outward from the ischium, and on account of inflammation the flesh tore at the joint, which was expelled from its seat.

P. 107.   *Certain Compositions Which Actually and Really Belong to Our Asclepiades*

Another poultice of Marcus Telentius Asclepiades,[389] very suitable for the same, especially beneficial for inflations of the uterus,

[386] Cael. Aurel. morb. acut. lib. III. 14. p. 224.

[387] Galen. de meth. med. lib. XIII. p. 173. T. IV. Here, according to Asclepiades, he calls inflammation "an obstruction or occlusion in theoretical interstices."

[388] This fragment was taken from Cocchi. script. chir. e collect. Nicet. p. 154. It is read also at the end of a book written by Cocchius (Dell 'anatomia discorso, d'Antonio Cocchi. Firenze MDCCXLV) Mention of it is also made by Conring in introd. p. 401 (ed. Helmst. 1687.) and Kestner im mediz. gelehrt. Lexicon s.v. (Jena, 1740.)

[389] vid. supr. cap. I. P. 2. not. k.

inscribed by him as an anodyne medication of Asclepiades because it is ascribed to the Bithynian as author.[390]

Three denaria of myrrh by weight, half a pound of all-heal by weight, half a pound of wax by weight, three ounces of galbanum by weight, half a pound of manna by weight, half a pound of guttammoniac by weight, half a pound of rubbed powdered resin by weight, half a sextarius of vinegar. It should be used as an anodyne also for all sympathetic nerve pain.

Celsus[391] has handed down to memory another medicine against all ailments of the ears, now approved by experience and compounded by Asclepiades. In it are one part each of cinnamon and cassia, two scruples each of flower of round bulrush, white castoreum, long pepper, amomum, and betelnut, and two parts each of male incense, Syrian nard, fat myrrh, saffron, and foam of saltpetre. These are separately pulverized, mixed again, mashed with vinegar, and so laid away; when it is to be used, it is diluted with vinegar.

P. 108.   *Use of the Onion, from the School of Asclepiades*

What is known to us about this we owe to Pliny, who speaks as follows: "The school of Asclepiades said that there is great benefit from this food for warmth. And if they daily eat it fasting, the security of their health is guarded: It is useful for the stomach, by stimulation of the spirit: it loosens and softens the bowels, dispels haemorrhoids, is a substitute for fruits and nuts: its juice with juice of fennel is wonderfully effective against incipient dropsies. Likewise against anginas, with rue and honey. And lethargics are stimulated by the same."[392]

P. 109.   *The Pulse According to the Sectarians of Asclepiades*

The pupils of Asclepiades add some details to their master's definition, so that theirs becomes that "the pulse is a dilation and contraction of the heart and arteries, which occurs not once in a single inspiration, but repeatedly." A corrector, by the name of Moschion*, declared that this motion is not merely in the heart and arteries,

---

[390] Galen. de composit. medic. sec. gen. lib. VII. p. 410. To. II.
[391] Cels. VI. 7.
[392] Plin. H. N. xx f. 20.
* Greek physician of second century, A.C., author of a book on gynaecology.

but also in the veins, in the brain, and in the membranes surrounding the latter.[393] (P. 61).

These are the items which, from the doctrine of the sectarians of Asclepiades I ought to bring forward in order that the teachings of Asclepiades himself may be better understood. Other things I keep silent, since they are plainly placed beyond the limits within which I am confined. They can better be treated in small articles which it is my purpose to write now that time is at hand, in which I shall show in what way from the doctrine of Asclepiades the sect of the Methodics arose. Perhaps, if I have leisure and opportunity, on the next occasion, when I have this matter straightened out, I shall communicate with learned men.

[393] Galen. de different. puls. lib. IV. p. 51. T. III.

Chapter IX

CONCLUSIONS

P. 110.   *He Calls the Dead Back to Life*

There remain a few points which could not be explained in the previous, foregoing sections. It seems sufficient, therefore, to devote this separate chapter to them.

Prominent among those things, which pertain to this, is that remarkable story through which we have ascertained that Asclepiades once recalled a dead man to life. It pleases us to hear Apuleius himself, who is copious and eloquent in narrating the affair:

"Asclepiades, when perchance he was going into the city, and returning from his suburban home in the country, observed a large funeral located in the outskirts of the city: standing around in a great multitude were many men who had come to the obsequies, all very sad and old-fashioned in their costume. He approached nearer, so that he even recognized, after the manner of humankind, who it was, since no one had answered him, as he lingered to ask: whether he himself should exercise any of his art on him? Certainly he restored life to the man lying there and almost buried. Contemplating diligently all the limbs of that wretch already sprinkled with perfumes, his face already smeared with sweet ointment, his body already washed and prepared for the funeral feast, Asclepiades observed by certain signs that he was alive. Again and again he palpated the man's body and found life latent in it. Immediately he exclaimed that the man was alive.

Therefore he urged that they should throw the torches far away, extinguish the fires, demolish the pyre, and take the funeral banquet back from the grave to the table. Meanwhile a murmur arose, partly to say that the doctor should be believed, partly also to ridicule him. Finally, though all his relatives were unwilling, whether because they themselves already had their inheritance or because thus far they had no faith in him, nevertheless with difficulty Asclepiades obtained a brief delay for the dead man, and so, snatching him from the hands of the pall-bearers, as if from the gods of the lower world, carried him home to his own house, and immediately revived his spirit: and immediately, with certain drugs, he restored the latent life to the recesses of his body."[394]

P. 111.   *The Monument of Asclepiades*

At the front of this book, we have taken care to have engraved the marble monument whereby Asclepiades is represented. Garofalo has commented on it in a separate book. The arguments, led by which he proves that the monument is a memorial to our Asclepiades, come to this: that, from the catalogue of men who have been distinguished by the same name of Asclepiades and which we have given above, he proves that none of them bore a more famous name than ours.

On the monument occurs merely the name Asclepiades. But we know that in the writings of Galen and others he was often called primarily Asclepiades. But anyone else of the same name, in order that the more easily, on account of being a less distinguished name, they might be differentiated from one another, was always designated by a cognomen, pronomen, or something else in them always celebrated in all places. Where Asclepiades occurs simply we should understand our philosopher and physician.

Garofalo derived another argument from the immense reputation of our man, which appears as much from his whole history as especially from the collected eulogies and praises of the writers above. (P. 21).

Then we think, if it is proved that that monument was sculptured before the century of Hadrian, as Garofalo infers from the absence of a beard, that there is no one of the Asclepiades to whom it could be ascribed, except our Bithynian, Pharmacion, and Philophysicus, who alone lived before that time, as we have shown above. But neither Pharmacion nor Philophysicus was so famous that, omitting our Bithynian, the monument could be assigned to either of them.[395]

P. 112.   *Asclepiades Explained the More Obscure Books of Hippocrates*

Already among the ancients there were those who devoted labor to expounding the books of Hippocrates, either all or only some of

---

[394] Apuleii Florid. IV. p. 276. In a few words the same story is told by Plin. H.N. VII. f. 37. XXVI. f. 8. and Cels. II. 6.

[395] Garofalo Giornal. de Letter. d'Ital. 1712. T. II. art. 10. et in dissert. miscell. p. 331. sq. Rom. 1718. 4. (Le Clerc Hist. de med. p. 410)

them. Also our Asclepiades wrote commentaries on Hippocrates, though not on all his books, but rather on those which from the outset were filled with obscurity. Galen, in his "Commentaries on Hippocrates," or whoever is author of this book, a work about the "office of medicine", reports some things from which it can be inferred for what reason he was engaged in explaining this book of Hippocrates.[396]

P. 113   *Athenaeus Confirms that Asclepiades was at Athens*

It is hardly to be doubted that Athenaeus is speaking of our Asclepiades, when he relates that Asclepiades the philosopher, while studying philosophic doctrines at Athens, was so indigent that he sought his livelihood in the bakeries, Athenaeus speaks thus:-

"Therefore summoning the philosophers Menedemos* and Asclepiades, who were young and impecunious, they asked them how, studying all day with the philosophers but earning nothing, they were in such good health in their bodies. And they bade a certain one of the millers to be summoned; and he came and said that they came down to the mill every night and ground and both received two drachmas. And the senators marvelled and gave them a reward of two hundred drachmas.[397]

P. 114.

Suidas, writing on Asclepiades relates that Apollonius was the teacher of Asclepiades Myrleanus. Hence no doubt Walsh was deceived that he calls our Asclepiades a pupil of Apollonius.

[396] Galen. comment in Hipp libr. de med. offic. p. 662. sqq. T. V.
[397] Athen. deipn. lib. IV. cap. XIX. p. 168. ed. Casaub.
* Pupil of Plato and founder of the Eretrian School.

INDEX

CPSIA information can be obtained
at www.ICGtesting.com
Printed in the USA
BVHW070846130820
586315BV00013B/509